WHY

PROPHET ELISHA

DIED SICK

AND
HOW TO AVOID IT

Amb Promise Ogbonna

WHY PROPHET ELISHA DIED SICK *AND HOW TO AVOID IT*
Copyright © August 2010 by
Amb Promise Ogbonna

Unless otherwise indicated, all Scriptural quotations are from the
New King James Version

In Nigeria, write *The Publisher:*
Ontop Life Publishers Company
Tel: +234 8060638053, +234 0853995257, +234 8027829586.
E-mail: ambpromiseo@gmail.com
Website: www.calm.org.ng.

YOU ARE WELCOME TO OUR SPECIAL SERVICES

Weekdays: 12:00-1:00pm. Hour of EmPowerment for All

***Saturdays**: 8:00-9:00am. Hour of Healing & Freedom for All*

***Sundays**: 8:00-9:00am. Hour of Liberty & Restoration for All*

***Sundays**: 9:00-10:00am. Hour of Kingdom Wealth Transfer to All*

***Last Friday Night Monthly:** 10:00pm. Night of Restorations for All*

***Ambassadors Bible Institute:** Trains and Releases Christ's Ambassadors on His Mission everywhere! Enroll today!*

Venue: 24 Independence Street, Behind O'Mark Schools by O'Mark Bus Stop, LASU Road, Igando Lagos.

DEDICATION

To You
And to all
Who hunger
And thirst for
God's best
In this generation!

CONTENTS

OUR HEAVENLY MANDATE

To Preach The Everlasting Gospel
To All everywhere,
Stop anything after man's destruction,
Bring Healing, Liberty and Restoration to all,

Raise, Build and Plant All as
Christ's Ambassadors on His Living Mission
Everywhere and Restore all things!

First Words

WHY PROPHET ELISHA DIED SICK AND HOW TO AVOID IT

God wants none of His Children to die sick, talk less of His Prophets. However, Prophet Elisha, one of the most anointed among God's Prophet died sick.

In His lifetime, Elisha raised the dead without speaking a word. He merely laid himself on the dead body twice and the dead rose up.

After his death, his dry bones raised back to life a dead man. Yet with all his anointing, he died sick. Why did he die sick?

The mystery behind his death through sickness is unraveled in this publication. It is not God's plan for you or anyone to end like Elisha. You can avoid it.

This book in your hands is a treasure. Guard it jealously. Study it diligently. Apply it purposefully. I see God's help has reached you at last. Make use of it and live. It is a new day for you in Jesus Name.

CHAPTER ONE

WAS SICKNESS GOD'S WILL FOR ELISHA?

Sickness is <u>never</u> God's plan for anyone. Sickness is not God's will for man.

No sickness is God's plan for any of His Children talkless of His Servants the Prophets. Therefore, sickness was not God's will for Elisha the Prophet.

However, Elisha was Sick. God says in the Scripture records that Elisha died sick.

If Sickness was not God's will for Elisha, God's own Prophet, how could he have died sick?

Well I asked God the same questions and many others. I asked because I needed an answer. I did not ask to justify the reason why any of His children should be sick and die premature like Elisha. I asked to get the answers so that I could avoid the mistake Elisha made and be able to live and fulfill my own destiny and equally help others live and not die sick.

The Lord God Almighty answered me and unfolded the truth in this book. It is for us to not to end like Elisha.

Beloved, sickness is not God's will. I want you to know you will not die sick no matter who and who died sick around you. Elisha might have died sick but you will not die sick even if your name is Elisha and you are also a Prophet. You will not die sick in Jesus Name.

This is so important for you to hear and believe; sickness was not God's will for Elisha nor for you. The Lord told me so and confirmed it for me from the Scriptures.

We shall look at few of them here.

Scriptural proofs to show Sickness was not God's will for Elisha.

1. Sin and Sickness are evil effects of man's fall and God does not want His Children to have them. He heals all He forgives and does not want any of his forgiven and healed children to be sick anymore.

Psalms 103:3
Who (God) forgives all your iniquities, Who heals all your diseases,

Isaiah 33:2
And the inhabitant will not say, "I am sick"; The people who dwell in it will be forgiven their iniquity.

2. Sickness is captivity and God does not want His Children to die in Captivity. Rather, He turns the captivity of people around by dealing with anything that caused it.

Job 2:4, 7
So Satan answered the LORD and said, "Skin for skin! Yes, all that a man has he will give for his life.
So Satan went out from the presence of the LORD, and struck Job with painful boils from the sole of his foot to the crown of his head.

Psalms 126:1-3 (KJV)
When the LORD turned again the captivity of Zion, we were like them that dream.
Then was our mouth filled with laughter, and our tongue with singing: then said they among the heathen, The LORD hath done great things for them.
The LORD hath done great things for us; whereof we are glad.

3. Sickness is bondage and God wants all Abraham Children set free from it. God who delivers his people from bondage using Prophets does not want them to die in bondage.

Luke 13:16

So ought not this woman, being a daughter of Abraham, whom Satan has bound--think of it--for eighteen years, be loosed from this bond on the Sabbath?

Hosea 12:13

And by a prophet the LORD brought Israel out of Egypt, and by a prophet was he preserved.

4. Sickness is from Satan and is called satanic oppression. And God went about in the person of Jesus doing good and healing all the sick oppressed by the devil.

Acts 10:38

How God anointed Jesus of Nazareth with the Holy Spirit and with power, who went about doing good and healing all who were oppressed by the devil, for God was with Him.

5. Sickness is a spirit of infirmity and is not for God's Children.

Luke 13:11-12

And behold, there was a woman who had a spirit of infirmity eighteen years, and was bent over and could in no way raise herself up.

But when Jesus saw her, He called her to Him and said to her, "Woman, you are loosed from your infirmity."

6. Sickness is a yoke and a burden. It binds one as a prisoner in confinement. God anointed Christ to destroy all the yokes.

Psalms 41:3

The LORD will strengthen him on his bed of illness; You will sustain him on his sickbed.

Isaiah 10:27

And it shall come to pass in that day, that his burden shall be taken away from off thy shoulder, and his yoke from off thy neck, and the yoke shall be destroyed because of the anointing.

James 5:14-15

Is anyone among you sick? Let him call for the elders of the church, and let them pray over him, anointing him with oil in the name of the Lord.

And the prayer of faith will save the sick, and the Lord will raise him up. And if he has committed sins, he will be forgiven.

7. Sickness is affliction, distress and destructions and is not meant for God's Children

Psalms 107:17, 19-20

Fools, because of their transgression, And because of their iniquities, were afflicted.

19 Then they cried out to the LORD in their trouble, And He saved them out of their distresses.

20 He sent His word and healed them, And delivered them from their destructions.

8. Sickness is the works of the devil. But God sent Jesus to destroy them.

1 John 3:8

He who sins is of the devil, for the devil has sinned from the beginning. For this purpose the Son of God was manifested, that He might destroy the works of the devil.

9. Sickness or Disease is a curse of the Law. God made Jesus a curse to free us from it.

Deuteronomy 28:20-21, 61

The LORD will send on you cursing, confusion, and rebuke in all that you set your hand to do, until you are destroyed and until you perish quickly, because of the wickedness of your doings in which you have forsaken Me.

The LORD will make the plague cling to you until He has consumed you from the land, which you are going to possess.

"Also every sickness and every plague, which is not written in this Book of the Law, will the LORD bring upon you until you are destroyed.

Galatians 3:13-14

Christ hath redeemed us from the curse of the law, being made a curse

That the blessing of Abraham might come on the Gentiles through Jesus Christ; that we might receive the promise of the Spirit through faith.

10. Sickness was not meant for God's Children – Israel, but for those who hate them.

Exodus 23:25-26

So you shall serve the LORD your God, and He will bless your bread and your water. And I will take sickness away from the midst of you.

No one shall suffer miscarriage or be barren in your land;
I will fulfill the number of your days.

Deuteronomy 7:14-15
You shall be blessed above all peoples; there shall not be a
male or female barren among you or among your
livestock.
And the LORD will take away from you all sickness, and
will afflict you with none of the terrible diseases of Egypt
which you have known, but will lay them on all those who
hate you.

(11) The Lord vowed to keep His Children who obey His
commandment healthy and cannot break His covenant nor
alter His word.
Exodus 15:26
And said, "If you diligently heed the voice of the LORD
your God and do what is right in His sight, give ear to His
commandments and keep all His statutes, I will put none of
the diseases on you which I have brought on the Egyptians.
For I am the LORD who heals you."
Psalms 89:34
My covenant will I not break, nor alter the thing that is
gone out of my lips.

12. God healed a heathen King with his entire family. Why
will sickness be His will for Elisha or any of His children?
Genesis 20:7, 17
Now therefore, restore the man's wife; for he is a prophet,
and he will pray for you and you shall live. But if you do
not restore her, know that you shall surely die, you and all
who are yours."

So Abraham prayed to God; and God healed Abimelech, his wife, and his female servants. Then they bore children;

13. Sickness is being under the power or control of a demon. God never wants any of His children to be under the power of any demon.

Mathew 8:16

16 When evening had come, they brought to Him many who were demon-possessed. And He cast out the spirits with a word, and healed all who were sick,

Mathew 9:32-33

As they went out, behold, they brought to Him a man, mute and demon-possessed.

And when the demon was cast out, the mute spoke. And the multitudes marveled, saying, "It was never seen like this in Israel!

14. Sickness is the surest way the thief – Satan, the devil robs, kills and destroys lives.

Psalms 107:17-19

Fools, because of their transgression, And because of their iniquities, were afflicted

Their soul abhorred all manner of food, And they drew near to the gates of death..

19 Then they cried out to the LORD in their trouble, And He saved them out of their distresses.

John 10:10

"The thief does not come except to steal, and to kill, and to destroy. I have come that they may have life, and that they may have it more abundantly.

15. Sickness brings untold suffering to people and if it was God's will then Jesus wouldn't have come to suffer for us in His flesh.

Luke 13:16

"So ought not this woman, being a daughter of Abraham, whom Satan has bound--think of it--for eighteen years, be loosed from this bond on the Sabbath?"

Mark 5:25-26

Now a certain woman had a flow of blood for twelve years,

And had suffered many things from many physicians. She had spent all that she had and was no better, but rather grew worse.

1Peter 4:1 *Therefore, since Christ suffered for us in the flesh, arm yourselves also with the same mind, for he who has suffered in the flesh has ceased from sin,*

16. Sickness is not God's will or else God would have been working against His own will when He came in the person of Jesus Christ His Son healing the sick.

John 6:38

For I have come down from heaven, not to do My own will, but the will of Him who sent Me.

John 14:10-11

Do you not believe that I am in the Father, and the Father in Me? The words that I speak to you I do not speak on My own authority; but the Father who dwells in Me does the works.

"Believe Me that I am in the Father and the Father in Me, or else believe Me for the sake of the works themselves.

Acts 10:38

How God anointed Jesus of Nazareth with the Holy Spirit and with power, who went about doing good and healing all who were oppressed by the devil, for God was with Him.

Beloved, God's will for man is healing, never his sickness. Therefore, it was not God's will for Elisha, His own chosen, empowered and sent Prophet to have been nor died sick. That is why He sent me: to tell you, 'You will not die sick' no matter the health challenge you might have now.

Prophet Elisha's story is for us to learn from, avoid his mistake and live.

Declare now:

I shall not die, but live, and declare the works of the LORD. Psalms 118:17

Regardless of the reason, it is not God's will for you to die sick. Therefore, you will live in Jesus Name.

CHAPTER TWO

WHY DID ELISHA FALL SICK

"Now when Elisha had fallen sick with the illness of which he was to die.....*2 Kings 13:14^A*

Elisha fell sick. God said *he fell* sick. People might not accept that but it is the truth. Let God be true and every man a liar.

Elisha's sickness was a fall. That shows very clearly he did not keep or maintain his position. God commands us to do all to stand. 'Having done all to stand, stand'. *Ephesians 6:13-14^A.*

God did not give Elisha the Sickness that eventually took his life. God does not need to kill anyone with sickness. He has all the power to do anything He wants. If He wants anyone dead anytime, He can take the person's life without necessarily doing so with sickness.

Scriptural proofs to show that Elisha could have died without sickness
1. No member of God's family (Zion) is to be sick.
Isaiah 33:24
And the inhabitant will not say, "I am sick"; The people who dwell in it will be forgiven their iniquity.

2. God has done all He needs to do to keep us healed.

Psalms 107: 20

He sent His word and healed them, and delivered them from their destructions.

3. Go has given us His own Ordained medicine for our health.
Proverbs 4:20-22

My son, give attention to my words; Incline your ear to my sayings.

Do not let them depart from your eyes; Keep them in the midst of your heart;

For they are life to those who find them, and health (medicine) to all their flesh.

4. The Lord is our Healer, Physician and Doctor. He wants us to hear and obey Him.
Exodus 15:26

And said, "If you diligently heed the voice of the LORD your God and do what is right in His sight, give ear to His commandments and keep all His statutes, I will put none of the diseases on you which I have brought on the Egyptians. For I am the LORD who heals you."

5. The Lord cannot fail to take away sickness from anyone who keeps His command.
Deuteronomy 7:11-15

Therefore, you shall keep the commandment, the statutes, and the judgments, which I command you today, to observe them.

Then it shall come to pass, because you listen to these judgments, and keep and do them, that the LORD your God will keep with you the covenant and the mercy which He swore to your fathers.

And He will love you and bless you and multiply you; He will also bless the fruit of your womb and the fruit of your land, your grain and your new wine and your oil, the increase of your cattle and the offspring of your flock, in the land of which He swore to your fathers to give you.

You shall be blessed above all peoples; there shall not be a male or female barren among you or among your livestock.

And the LORD will take away from you all sickness, and will afflict you with none of the terrible diseases of Egypt which you have known, but will lay them on all those who hate you.

6. The Lord services the health needs of His servants.
Exodus 23:25-26
So you shall serve the LORD your God, and He will bless your bread and your water. And I will take sickness away from the midst of you.

No one shall suffer miscarriage or be barren in your land; I will fulfill the number of your days.

Psalms 91:16
With long life I will satisfy him, and show him My salvation.

I want to make it very clear that My Father never afflicted Elisha the Prophet with sickness that led to his death. That sickness was from the devil. God gives only good gifts and sickness is not a good gift.

James 1:17
Every good gift and every perfect gift is from above, and comes down from the Father of lights, with whom there is no variation or shadow of turning.

20

Sickness is not a good gift. Sickness is an evil, destructive spirit called "spirit of infirmity" or spirit sickness is never from God

Luke 13:11, 16

"And behold, there was a woman who had a spirit of infirmity eighteen years, and was bent over and could in no way raise herself up.

So ought not this woman, being a daughter of Abraham, whom Satan has bound--think of it--for eighteen years, be loosed from this bond on the Sabbath?"

God, My Father is called "I am that I am.*" Exodus 3:14.* He cannot change. He has not changed and can never change.

If He can give sickness today then you can believe He gave Elisha   sickness. If He healed before, it is to show His will that He does not want anyone to be or die sick.

God says, "I will put none of the diseases of Egypt on you but will lay them on those who hate you." He does not give anyone sickness because He only gives good gifts and there is no variableness with Him.

There is permissive and causative cause.

Someone can permit something to happen. While another can cause something to happen.

God does not afflict anyone with disease or sickness but He can allow or permit anyone to be afflicted with sickness.

Please hear me: God does not cause or smite His Children with disease or sickness. He can allow or permit them (His children) to be afflicted with sickness when they choose to go their own way.

Why will God Permit or Allow His Children to be afflicted with Sickness or Disease?

Remember God is the "I AM". That means He is forever the same in the past, in the present, in the future. His way today has been His way since the beginning and will remain His way forever.

Why did God allow Elisha to be smitten with sickness that led to His death?

1. God does nothing on earth without telling his prophet.
Amos 3:7
Surely the Lord GOD does nothing, Unless He reveals His secret to His servants the prophets.
Elisha as God's prophets knew the Covenant abhors sickness yet he allowed himself to get sick when he could have stopped it.
Mathew 16:19
"And I will give you the keys of the kingdom of heaven, and whatever you bind on earth will be bound in heaven, and whatever you loose on earth will be loosed in heaven."

2. God allows on earth anything we allow. We make the choice and God backs us up.
Mathew 18:18
Assuredly, I say to you, whatever you bind on earth will be bound in heaven, and whatever you loose on earth will be loosed in heaven.
If you believe God's Word to be true, then Elisha allowed the enemy to strike him with sickness on earth and God in heaven could not do anything about it.

Had Elisha desired it otherwise, it could have been so for him.

3. God disallows anything we disallow.
Isaiah 38:1-5
In those days Hezekiah was sick and near death. And Isaiah the prophet, the son of Amoz, went to him and said to him, "Thus says the LORD: 'Set your house in order, for you shall die and not live.'"

Then Hezekiah turned his face toward the wall, and prayed to the LORD,

And said, "Remember now, O LORD, I pray, how I have walked before You in truth and with a loyal heart, and have done what is good in Your sight." And Hezekiah wept bitterly.

And the word of the LORD came to Isaiah, saying,

Go and tell Hezekiah, 'Thus says the LORD, the God of David your father: "I have heard your prayer, I have seen your tears; surely I will add to your days fifteen years.

King Hezekiah did not allow himself to die even when God said so. God who by himself said He would die could not go ahead to perform what he said because Hezekiah did not permit his death.

Hear me: if Hezekiah could make God stop his sickness and God's sentence of death on him also, then Elisha had every reason to have stopped himself from becoming sick in the first place talkless of dying by it.

Elisha the Prophet fell sick and died because he allowed himself to be sick.

4. Elisha was a man of great insight and revelation and so had enough insight to know God does not give His Children sickness nor does He want them to die sick.

2 Kings 8:7-10

Then Elisha went to Damascus, and Ben-Hadad king of Syria was sick; and it was told him, saying, "The man of God has come here."

And the king said to Hazael, "Take a present in your hand, and go to meet the man of God, and inquire of the LORD by him, saying, 'Shall I recover from this disease?'"

So Hazael went to meet him and took a present with him, of every good thing of Damascus, forty camel-loads; and he came and stood before him, and said, "Your son Ben-Hadad king of Syria has sent me to you, saying, 'Shall I recover from this disease?'"

And Elisha said to him, "Go, say to him, 'You shall certainly recover.' However the LORD has shown me that he will really die."

Elisha told a king who made wars against Israel he will recover of his sickness. Why would He (God) allow Elisha die sick? Therefore, he could have stopped sickness from destroying his life, just as he stopped Naaman from dying a leper (2 Kings 5:1, 9, 10, 14)

5. Elisha was also a man of faith. The just lives by faith and stops all enemy vices, forces and attacks by faith.

Habakkuk 2:4

"Behold the proud, His soul is not upright in him; But the just shall live by his faith.

That means, the proud the unjust and the faithless suffer or die.

Ephesians 6:16
Above all, taking the shield of faith with which you will be able to quench all the fiery darts of the wicked one.

Mathew 9:28-29
And when He had come into the house, the blind men came to Him. And Jesus said to them, "Do you believe that I am able to do this?" They said to Him, "Yes, Lord."
Then He touched their eyes, saying, "According to your faith let it be to you."

Mathew 8:13
Then Jesus said to the centurion, "Go your way; and as you have believed, so let it be done for you." And his servant was healed that same hour.

Elisha had faith that an axe-head could swim and it did when he took a tree branch and cast it into the river (2 kings 6:5-7). He was a man of faith. However, when sickness came to him, he died. The just shall live. If Elisha did not, from Habakkuk 2:4, three things were responsible – Pride, being unjust and lack of faith. Please, take heed to thyself and fear God no matter who you are.

You won't die like Elisha. That is why this revelation.
Please hear me: Elisha fell sick not because God caused his sickness but because he (Elisha) permitted or allowed it by not taking his place of authority as a god and ruler over all creatures on the earth.

If you are sick today, whether you are a Christian, Churchgoer or an unbeliever, you allowed it. You are the cause of your sickness. Satan cannot impose anything on anyone but the ignorant and the unbelievers, whether in the "Church" or in God's family or outside.

This is the truth you must know and tell yourself if you want to live and not end like Elisha. It is the key that unlocks the door to your healing and recovery.

1. God's man has the final say on earth.
God has given His Children the power and authority to decide what happen on this earth but most fail to use them when they need to.

Genesis 2:15
Then the LORD God took the man and put him in the Garden of Eden to tend and keep it.
God told Adam to till Eden and to keep it. Man's failure to keep what he was empowered and commissioned to keep caused problems in Eden. The same is what is causing problem for man in every generation.
Psalms 8:3-6
When I consider Your heavens, the work of
Your fingers, The moon and the stars, which You have ordained,
What is man that You are mindful of him, And the son of man that You visit him?
For You have made him a little lower than the angels, And You have crowned him with glory and honor.
You have made him to have dominion over the works of Your hands; You have put all things under his feet

2. God's man is in total control of everything here on earth, but can only function effectively under God.
James 4:27
Therefore submit to God. Resist the devil and he will flee from you.

3. God's – Man can only function here on earth as God ordained by faith.
Ephesians 6:16
Above all, taking the shield of faith with which you will be able to quench all the fiery darts of the wicked one.

4. God's man is to give no place to the devil. We are to stop him always.
Ephesians 4:27
Nor give place to the devil.

5. God's man is to go about setting free the oppressed.
Acts 10:38
"How God anointed Jesus of Nazareth with the Holy Spirit and with power, who went about doing good and healing all who were oppressed by the devil, for God was with Him.

Jesus, a Prophet stopped sickness. Had Elisha taken the shield of faith, he could have either stopped the sickness or enforced his healing. God was not responsible for Elisha's sickness and death and must not be blamed nor accused for anyone's sickness and death.
Elisha failed to take responsibility when he was attacked with sickness and so he died.

Recall he raised a dead person back to life. Elisha did not say a word. He merely stretched himself on the boy's dead body twice and raised the dead.

2 Kings 4:32-36

When Elisha came into the house, there was the child, lying dead on his bed.

He went in therefore, shut the door behind the two of them, and prayed to the LORD.

And he went up and lay on the child, and put his mouth on his mouth, his eyes on his eyes, and his hands on his hands; and he stretched himself out on the child, and the flesh of the child became warm.

He returned and walked back and forth in the house, and again went up and stretched himself out on him; then the child sneezed seven times, and the child opened his eyes.

And he called Gehazi and said, "Call this Shunammite woman." So he called her. And when she came in to him, he said, "Pick up your son."

Elisha permitted his death. God did not

Another reason for Elisha's sickness is that he operated alone after his servant left him.

Ecclesiastes 4:9

9 Two are better than one, Because they have a good reward for their labor.

A curse of "woe" is the portion of anyone who operates alone.

Jesus got at least six disciples when he started his ministry, then he later chose the twelve. Jesus had a team.

Mathew 4:17-19

From that time, Jesus began to preach and to say, "Repent, for the kingdom of heaven is at hand."

And Jesus, walking by the Sea of Galilee, saw two brothers, Simon called Peter, and Andrew his brother, casting a net into the sea; for they were fishermen.

Then He said to them, "Follow Me, and I will make you fishers of men."

John 1:43

The following day Jesus wanted to go to Galilee, and He found Philip and said to him, "Follow Me."

Mark 3:13-14

And He went up on the mountain and called to Him those He Himself wanted. And they came to Him.

Then He appointed twelve, that they might be with Him and that He might send them out to preach,

Operating alone in ministry has grave consequences. Elisha suffered because of it.

Overwork results naturally, when one is working alone. Moses was advised against operating alone.

Exodus 18:17-18

So Moses' father-in-law said to him, "The thing that you do is not good.

"Both you and these people who are with you will surely wear yourselves out. For this thing is too much for you; you are not able to perform it by yourself.

Paul had people he worked with.

Philippians 2:25-27

Yet I considered it necessary to send to you Epaphroditus, my brother, fellow worker, and fellow soldier, but your messenger and the one who ministered to my need;

Since he was longing for you all, and was distressed because you had heard that he was sick.

For indeed he was sick almost unto death; but God had mercy on him, and not only on him but on me also, lest I should have sorrow upon sorrow.

Overwork is a possible cause of sickness and death as it almost cost Epaphroditus death.

David Yonggi Cho almost died from an illness because of overwork.

Robert Murray Mccheyne died at 29 years because of illness that came upon him as a result of overwork. On his death bed, he lamented before he passed on that "God gave him a message and a horse (his body) to deliver the message. He killed the horse (his body) and couldn't deliver the message"

The work of ministry is a very serious, tasking job and so does not require lone-operators.

Making a wrong move or relocating except at God's command causes mishap. Every minister must abide in his place of primary assignment. Elisha left Mount Carmel and went to Damascus after he prophesied about the seven years of famine.

2 Kings 8:1, 7

Then Elisha spoke to the woman whose son he had restored to life, saying, "Arise and go, you and your household, and stay wherever you can; for the LORD has called for a famine, and furthermore, it will come upon the land for seven years."

Then Elisha went to Damascus, and Ben-Hadad king of Syria was sick; and it was told him, saying, "The man of God has come here."

Before Elijah went to the Brook Cherith or to Zarepheth it was at God's command, (1 Kings17:2-3,7-9).

There is no record God sent Elisha to Damascus. He just got up and went to wherever he could after his advice to the woman to do the same (2 Kings 8:1).

Getting up and going just where you like is an exhibition of self-will and is not for ministers (see John 21:18; Roman 8:14)

Elisha went on his own leading and was not able to return to his base before his death. Carmel is on the Southern part of Israel close to Bethlehem (which means, 'The House of Bread') but he moved to Damascus in Syria far Northeast. He lived in isolation from God's people that he was meant to oversee and minister to.

Elimelech relocated wrongly and died with his two sons leaving his wife, Naomi and Ruth and Orpah, their son's wives, as widows in a strange land. I can bet you sickness killed them, although it was not stated in the Bible. It was not hunger or poverty else, the wives would have died.

Ruth 1:1-5

Now it came to pass, in the days when the judges ruled, that there was a famine in the land. And a certain man of Bethlehem, Judah, went to dwell in the country of Moab, he and his wife and his two sons.

The name of the man was Elimelech, the name of his wife was Naomi, and the names of his two sons were Mahlon and Chilion-Ephrathites of Bethlehem, Judah. And they went to the country of Moab and remained

Then Elimelech, Naomi's husband, died; and she was left, and her two sons.

Now they took wives of the women of Moab: the name of the one was Orpah, and the name of the other Ruth. And they dwelt there about ten years.

Then both Mahlon and Chilion also died; so the woman survived her two sons and her husband.

God has an appointed time for His own where He secure them always.

2 Samuel 7:10

"Moreover I will appoint a place for My people Israel, and will plant them, that they may dwell in a place of their own and move no more; nor shall the sons of wickedness oppress them anymore, as previously,

Affliction, sickness or oppression only comes when we transgress or derail.

Psalms 119:67

Before I was afflicted I went astray, But now I keep Your word.

Psalms 107:17-20

Fools, because of their transgression, And because of their iniquities, were afflicted.

Their soul abhorred all manner of food, And they drew near to the gates of death.

Then they cried out to the LORD in their trouble, And He saved them out of their distresses.

He sent His word and healed them, And delivered them from their destructions.

The enemy afflicts God's people when they move out of their God-ordained place. Sickness is an affliction of the devil.

The afflicted when they call on the Lord in repentance are healed and delivered. Why must Elisha die if he did call God in repentance?

Elisha demonstrated anger, a very negative emotion which springs out of resentment and bitterness. Bitterness defiles a man and leaves him vulnerable to satanic attacks.

2 Kings 13:18-21
Then he said, "Take the arrows"; so he took them. And he said to the king of Israel, "Strike the ground"; so he struck three times, and stopped.
And the man of God was angry with him, and said, "You should have struck five or six times; then you would have struck Syria till you had destroyed it! But now you will strike Syria only three times."
Then Elisha died, and they buried him. And the raiding bands from Moab invaded the land in the spring of the year.
So it was, as they were burying a man, that suddenly they spied a band of raiders; and they put the man in the tomb of Elisha; and when the man was let down and touched the bones of Elisha, he revived and stood on his feet.

Ecclesiastes 7:9, 17
Do not hasten in your spirit to be angry, For anger rests in the bosom of fools.
Do not be overly wicked, Nor be foolish: Why should you die before your time?

Anger rests in the bosom of fools and fools die before their time because anger releases poisonous toxic substances into their system that breaks down their physical metabolism causing sickness and other body ailments.

Unforgiveness is another reason that led to Elisha's sickness and eventual death. Unforgiveness and bitterness are deadly killers because they leave you on your own, without God's divine security.

When Naaman was healed, he offered Elisha a gift. Elisha rejected it. Later, Gehazi, Elisha's servant went after Naaman and collected the gift claiming Elisha sent him. Elisha knew and cursed Gehazi and his generations *forever.*

2 Kings 5:14-15, 20-27
So he went down and dipped seven times in the Jordan, according to the saying of the man of God; and his flesh was restored like the flesh of a little child, and he was clean.
And he returned to the man of God, he and all his aides, and came and stood before him; and he said, "Indeed, now I know that there is no God in all the earth, except in Israel; now therefore, please take a gift from your servant."
But Gehazi, the servant of Elisha the man of God, said, "Look, my master has spared Naaman this Syrian, while not receiving from his hands what he brought; but as the LORD lives, I will run after him and take something from him."
So Gehazi pursued Naaman. When Naaman saw him running after him, he got down from the chariot to meet him, and said, "Is all well?"
And he said, "All is well. My master has sent me, saying, 'Indeed, just now two young men of the sons of the prophets have come to me from the mountains of Ephraim. Please give them a talent of silver and two changes of garments.'"

So Naaman said, "Please, take two talents." And he urged him, and bound two talents of silver in two bags, with two changes of garments, and handed them to two of his servants; and they carried them on ahead of him.

When he came to the citadel, he took them from their hand, and stored them away in the house; then he let the men go, and they departed.

Now he went in and stood before his master. Elisha said to him, "Where did you go, Gehazi?" And he said, "Your servant did not go anywhere."

Then he said to him, "Did not my heart go with you when the man turned back from his chariot to meet you? Is it time to receive money and to receive clothing, olive groves and vineyards, sheep and oxen, male and female servants?

Therefore the leprosy of Naaman shall cling to you and your descendants forever." And he went out from his presence leprous, as white as snow.

Elisha had every reason to be angry. He also had every reason to have forgiven his servant or even spared his children and generations forever. But he cursed him and his seed forever.

Hebrews 12:12-13
Therefore, strengthen the hands, which hang down, and the feeble knees,
And make straight paths for your feet, so that what is lame may not be dislocated, but rather be healed.

Mathew 6:14-15
For if you forgive men their trespasses, your heavenly Father will also forgive you.
But if you do not forgive men their trespasses, neither will your Father forgive your trespasses.

Mark 11:23-25

For assuredly, I say to you, whoever says to this mountain, 'Be removed and be cast into the sea,' and does not doubt in his heart, but believes that those things he says will be done, he will have whatever he says.

Therefore I say to you, whatever things you ask when you pray, believe that you receive them, and you will have them.

And whenever you stand praying, if you have anything against anyone, forgive him, that your Father in heaven may also forgive you your trespasses.

Even if every other reason could have been overlooked, God cannot overlooked this – unforgiveness.

Ecclesiastes 7:20

For there is not a just man on earth who does good And does not sin.

Elisha could have forgiven Gahazi. It is not impossible he prayed while sick, yet died. Why? Unforgiveness and judgment against others destroy.

God's wise counsel to His own people.

Luke 17:3-4

Take heed to yourselves. If your brother sins against you, rebuke him; and if he repents, forgive him.

"And if he sins against you seven times in a day, and seven times in a day returns to you, saying, 'I repent,' you shall forgive him."

Mathew 18:15, 21-35

Moreover if your brother sins against you, go and tell him his fault between you and him alone. If he hears you, you have gained your brother.

Then Peter came to Him and said, "Lord, how often shall my brother sin against me, and I forgive him? Up to seven times?"

Jesus said to him, "I do not say to you, up to seven times, but up to seventy times seven.

Therefore the kingdom of heaven is like a certain king who wanted to settle accounts with his servants.

And when he had begun to settle accounts, one was brought to him who owed him ten thousand talents.

But as he was not able to pay, his master commanded that he be sold, with his wife and children and all that he had, and that payment be made.

The servant therefore fell down before him, saying, 'Master, have patience with me,

and I will pay you all.'

Then the master of that servant was moved with compassion, released him, and forgave him the debt.

"But that servant went out and found one of his fellow servants who owed him a hundred denarii; and he laid hands on him and took him by the throat, saying, 'Pay me what you owe!'

So his fellow servant fell down at his feet and begged him, saying, 'Have patience with me, and I will pay you all.'

And he would not, but went and threw him into prison till he should pay the debt.

So when his fellow servants saw what had been done, they were very grieved, and came and told their master all that had been done.

Then his master, after he had called him, said to him, 'You wicked servant! I forgave you all that debt because you begged me.

Should you not also have had compassion on your fellow servant, just as *I* had pity on you?'

And his master was angry, and delivered him to the torturers until he should pay all that was due to him.

So My heavenly Father also will do to you if each of you, from his heart, does not forgive his brother his trespasses."

Luke 6:37-38

Judge not, and you shall not be judged. Condemn not, and you shall not be condemned. Forgive, and you will be forgiven.

Give, and it will be given to you: good measure, pressed down, shaken together, and running over will be put into your bosom. For with the same measure that you use, it will be measured back to you."

Elisha had every reason to have been healed if he chose to and did what was right in God's sight. But he blew it and paid for it.

God is no respecter of persons. Elisha's life is clearly shown in God's Word for you and me to learn from.

Romans 15:4

For whatever things were written before were written for our learning, that we through the patience and comfort of the Scriptures might have hope.

1 Corinthians 10:11

Now all these things happened to them as examples, and they were written for our admonition, upon whom the ends of the ages have come.

The position we occupy is to help us serve God better. Live by the Word and live. Elisha died sick. But you can avoid his mistakes and secure your healing today and now. Sickness is from the devil. It is God's will to heal all who are sick no matter what caused their sickness. You are not to die by sickness.

Therefore, 'You will not die but live' in Jesus name.

CHAPTER THREE

WHY DIDN'T GOD HEAL ELISHA?

God wants to heal all the sick even you no matter your sickness, its cause and how long it has lasted.

Healing is a good gift from God.

James 1:17
Every good gift and every perfect gift is from above, and comes down from the Father of lights, with whom there is no variation or shadow of turning.

Healing is God's will.

John 6:38
For I have come down from heaven, not to do My own will, but the will of Him who sent Me.
Healing is doing good and is God's duty and work.
Acts 10:38
How God anointed Jesus of Nazareth with the Holy Spirit and with power, who went about doing good and healing all who were oppressed by the devil, for God was with Him.

God gives it to all the sick who desire it. God also heals even those who believe Him to heal their loved ones.

Proverbs 10:24

The fear of the wicked will come upon him, And the desire of the righteous will be granted.
Psalms 145:14-16, 19
The LORD upholds all who fall, And raises up all who are bowed down.
The eyes of all look expectantly to You, And You give them their food in due season.
You open Your hand And satisfy the desire of every living thing.
He will fulfill the desire of those who fear Him; He also will hear their cry and save them.

Whether you are born again or not, God's desire is to heal all who obey His divine instructions or seek Him to be healed.

SCRIPTURAL CASES TO PROVE GOD HEALS ALL WHO DO AS HE SAYS.
Case 1: God healed king Abimelech
"Now therefore, restore the man's wife; for he is a prophet, and he will pray for you and you shall live. But if you do not restore her, know that you shall surely die, you and all who are yours."
So Abraham prayed to God; and God healed Abimelech, his wife, and his female servants. Then they bore children.Genesis 20:7, 17

A heathen king, Abimelech was healed with his entire family because he heard and obeyed God's divine instructions.

Case 2: God healed king Benhadad

Then Elisha went to Damascus, and Ben-Hadad king of Syria was sick; and it was told him, saying, "The man of God has come here."

And the king said to Hazael, "Take a present in your hand, and go to meet the man of God, and inquire of the LORD by him, saying, 'Shall I recover from this disease?'"

So Hazael went to meet him and took a present with him, of every good thing of Damascus, forty camel-loads; and he came and stood before him, and said, "Your son Ben-Hadad king of Syria has sent me to you, saying, 'Shall I recover from this disease?'"

And Elisha said to him, "Go, say to him, 'You shall certainly recover.' However the LORD has shown me that he will really die."

Then he departed from Elisha, and came to his master, who said to him, What did Elisha say to you?" And he answered, "He told me you would surely recover." 2 Kings 8:7-10, 14

Ben-hadad King of Syria was sick and sought God by inquiring from Elisha who told him he will recover but will be killed by the servant Hazael. It was not sickness that killed Ben-hadad because he sought God.

Case 3: God healed a Centurion's servant
And a certain centurion's servant, who was dear to him, was sick and ready to die.

So when he heard about Jesus, he sent elders of the Jews to Him, pleading with Him to come and heal his servant.

And those who were sent, returning to the house, found the servant well who had been sick. . Luke 7:2-3, 10

A centurion whose servant was sick and ready to die received healing because he sought Jesus.

Case 4: God Healed a Gentile Woman's daughter
For a woman whose young daughter had an unclean spirit heard about Him, and she came and fell at His feet.
The woman was a Greek, a Syro-Phoenician by birth, and she kept asking Him to cast the demon out of her daughter.
But Jesus said to her, "Let the children be filled first, for it is not good to take the children's bread and throw it to the little dogs."
And she answered and said to Him, "Yes, Lord, yet even the little dogs under the table eat from the children's crumbs."
Then He said to her, "For this saying goes your way; the demon has gone out of your daughter."
And when she had come to her house, she found the demon gone out, and her daughter lying on the bed. Mark 7:25-30

A Greek woman's daughter who was under satanic torture got healed and delivered because the mother sought Jesus.

Case 5: God Healed a nobleman's son
So Jesus came again to Cana of Galilee where He had made the water wine. And there was a certain nobleman whose son was sick at Capernaum.
When he heard that Jesus had come out of Judea into Galilee, he went to Him and implored Him to come down and heal his son, for he was at the point of death.
The nobleman said to Him, "Sir, come down before my child dies!"

Jesus said to him, "Go your way; your son lives." So the man believed the word that Jesus spoke to him, and he went his way.

And as he was now going down, his servants met him and told him, saying, "Your son lives!" John 4:46-47, 49-51

The nobleman's son who was at the point of death got healed because he sought the Lord for his son's healing.

Case 6: <u>God Healed king Hezekiah</u>

In those days Hezekiah was sick and near death. And Isaiah the prophet, the son of Amoz, went to him and said to him, "Thus says the LORD: 'Set your house in order, for you shall die, and not live.'"

Then he turned his face toward the wall, and prayed to the LORD, saying,

"Remember now, O LORD, I pray, how I have walked before You in truth and with a loyal heart, and have done what was good in Your sight." And Hezekiah wept bitterly.

And it happened, before Isaiah had gone out into the middle court, that the word of the LORD came to him, saying,

"Return and tell Hezekiah the leader of My people, 'Thus says the LORD, the God of David your father: "I have heard your prayer, I have seen your tears; surely I will heal you. On the third day you shall go up to the house of the LORD. 2Kings 20:1-5

Hezekiah was sick unto death and God sent prophet Isaiah to him telling him to put his house in order for he was going to die. He sought God and was healed.

Case 7:<u>God Healed Epaphrodititus</u>

Yet I considered it necessary to send to you Epaphroditus, my brother, fellow worker, and fellow soldier, but your messenger and the one who ministered to my need;

Since he was longing for you all, and was distressed because you had heard that he was sick.

For indeed he was sick almost unto death; but God had mercy on him, and not only on him but on me also, lest I should have sorrow upon sorrow. Philippians 2:25-27

God had mercy and healed *Epaphroditus* who was sick to the point of death. From those seven points above, it is very clear that God heats all that sought him while sick.

God is no respecter of persons. He responds to all who desire and seek Him for His blessings.

If God ever healed anyone before, He can do so now and forever, for whoever will believe and obey His word.

<u>Acts 10:34-35</u>

Then Peter opened his mouth and said: "In truth I perceive that God shows no partiality.

But in every nation whoever fears Him and works righteousness is accepted by Him.

<u>Romans 10:10-12</u>

For with the heart one believes unto righteousness and with the mouth confession is made unto salvation.

For the Scripture says, "Whoever believes on Him will not be put to shame."

For there is no distinction between Jew and Greek, for the same Lord over all is rich to all who call upon Him.

God does not give any special attention to anyone who ignores His Word. It is either you obey God or you suffer. Even Jesus learnt this

Jesus suffered until he learnt how to obey God.
Hebrews 5:7-8
Who, in the days of His flesh, when He had offered up prayers and supplications, with vehement cries and tears to Him who was able to save Him from death, and was heard because of His godly fear,
Though He was a Son, yet He learned obedience by the things which He suffered.

God is not going to do anything for anyone who refuses to ask Him for it.

Every father gives food, healthcare and every other good gifts to his children.

"If a son asks for bread from any father among you, will he give him a stone? Or if he asks for a fish, will he give him a serpent instead of a fish?
Or if he asks for an egg, will he offer him a scorpion?
If you then, being evil, know how to give good gifts to your children, how much more will your heavenly Father give the Holy Spirit to those who ask Him! Luke 11:11-13

Therefore submit to God. Resist the devil and he will flee from you.
Draw near to God and He will draw near to you. Cleanse your hands, you sinners; and purify your hearts, you double-minded. James 4:7-8

God responds to all who draw nigh to Him and to those who sit back and do nothing

Job 22:21-23, 28-30

Now acquaint yourself with Him, and be at peace; Thereby good will comes to you.

Receive, please, instruction from His mouth, And lay up His words in your heart.

If you return to the Almighty, you will be built up; You will remove iniquity far from your tents.

God is open to all who seek Him and always ensure their needs are met.

Jeremiah 29:13

And you will seek Me and find Me, when you search for Me with all your heart.

Psalms 34:10

The young lions lack and suffer hunger; But those who seek the LORD shall not lack any good thing.

Psalms 84:11

For the LORD God is a sun and shield; The LORD will give grace and glory; No good thing will He withhold From those who walk uprightly.

God withholds nothing from all who seek Him for His blessings. Healing is the children's bread. God cannot withhold healing from any of His children.

Proverbs 3:27-28

27 Do not withhold good from those to whom it is due, When it is in the power of your hand to do so.

28 Do not say to your neighbor, "Go, and come back, And tomorrow I will give it," When you have it with you.

God has the power to heal all who come to Him and cannot tell anyone to go and come next time when He has right now all it takes to heal any kind of sickness or disease.

DEATH IS THE PENALTY TO THE SICK WHO IGNORED GOD

The same way all that came seeking the Lord were healed, all who go seeking man when sick suffered and died eventually.

Scriptural proofs to show this truth
 1. Jeremiah 8:20, 22
The harvest is past, the summer is ended, and we are not saved!
Is there no balm in Gilead, Is there no physician there? Why then is there no recovery for the health of the daughter of my people?
All who went elsewhere for healing did not recover. There was no healing because God was not sought

 2. Jeremiah 30:13
13 There is no one to plead your cause, that you may be bound up; You have no healing medicines.
There is no healing medicine made by man that will heal. Neither was there cures after taking all man-made medicines.

 3. Jeremiah 46:11
Go up to Gilead and take balm, O virgin, the daughter of Egypt; In vain you will use many medicines; You shall not be cured.

The sick that sought men suffered.

4. <u>Mark 5:25-26</u>
Now a certain woman had a flow of blood for twelve years, And had suffered many things from many physicians. She had spent all that she had and was no better, but rather grew worse.
The one who sough men died.

5. <u>2 King 1:2-4, 16-17</u>
Now Ahaziah fell through the lattice of his upper room in Samaria, and was injured; so he sent messengers and said to them, "Go, inquire of Baal-Zebub, the god of Ekron, whether I shall recover from this injury."
But the angel of the LORD said to Elijah the Tishbite, "Arise, go up to meet the messengers of the king of Samaria, and say to them, 'Is it because there is no God in Israel that you are going to inquire of Baal-Zebub, the god of Ekron?'
Now therefore, thus says the LORD: 'You shall not come down from the bed to which you have gone up, but you shall surely die.'" So Elijah departed.
Then he said to him, "Thus says the LORD: 'Because you have sent messengers to inquire of Baal-Zebub, the god of Ekron, is it because there is no God in Israel to inquire of His word? Therefore you shall not come down from the bed to which you have gone up, but you shall surely die.'"
So Ahaziah died according to the word of the LORD which Elijah had spoken. Because he had no son, Jehoram became king in his place, in the second year of Jehoram the son of Jehoshaphat, king of Judah.

The King did not enquire from God and so died according to God's word.

To ignore God by the sick and seek man shows utter disregard and contempt toward your creator and has caused the death of so many preachers and God's servants.

It is God's will to heal all the sick. Elisha knew it. If it was God's will for one man to be healed of his sickness it is God's will for all men to be healed of their sicknesses. If it was God's will for two people to recover from their sickness, then it is an established fundamental truth that God wants all people to recover from all their sicknesses no matter the cause.

Therefore, it is God's will for Elisha to have been healed and to have recovered from his illness in spite of the cause, but he did not.

So why didn't God heal Elisha?

All the factors considered in the previous chapter contributed but I left out a major contributor to his eventual death. Let us look at God's Word.

1 Kings 19:15-17, 19-21

Then the LORD said to him: "Go, return on your way to the Wilderness of Damascus; and when you arrive, anoint Hazael as king over Syria.

Also you shall anoint Jehu the son of Nimshi as king over Israel. And Elisha the son of Shaphat of Abel Meholah you shall anoint as prophet in your place.

It shall be that whoever escapes the sword of Hazael, Jehu will kill; and whoever escapes the sword of Jehu, Elisha will kill.

So he departed from there, and found Elisha the son of Shaphat, who was plowing with twelve yoke of oxen before him, and he was with the twelfth. Then Elijah passed by him and threw his mantle on him.

And he left the oxen and ran after Elijah, and said, "Please let me kiss my father and my mother, and then I will follow you." And he said to him, Go back again, for what have I done to you?"

So Elisha turned back from him, and took a yoke of oxen and slaughtered them and boiled their flesh, using the oxen's equipment, and gave it to the people, and they ate. Then he arose and followed Elijah, and became his servant.

The Lord's command to Elijah was
  - Anoint Hazael king over Syria
  - Anoint Jehu king over Israel
  - Anoint Elisha as a prophet in your place.

Elijah only went to Elisha his replacement because he knew he will do all God commanded him to do if he is gone.

Elijah went to heaven without anointing Hazael as king over Syria and Jehu king over Israel.

Normally, Elisha, having taken over from Elijah officially was saddled with that responsibility but he did not do it.

<u>2 Kings 8:7-13</u>

Then Elisha went to Damascus, and Ben-Hadad king of Syria was sick; and it was told him, saying, "The man of God has come here."

And the king said to Hazael, "Take a present in your hand, and go to meet the man of God, and inquire of the LORD by him, saying, 'Shall I recover from this disease?'"

So Hazael went to meet him and took a present with him, of every good thing of Damascus, forty camel-loads; and he came and stood before him, and said, "Your son Ben-Hadad king of Syria has sent me to you, saying, 'Shall I recover from this disease?'"

And Elisha said to him, "Go, say to him, 'You shall certainly recover.' However the LORD has shown me that he will really die."

Then he set his countenance in a stare until he was ashamed; and the man of God wept.

And Hazael said, "Why is my lord weeping?" He answered, "Because I know the evil that you will do to the children of Israel: Their strongholds you will set on fire, and their young men you will kill with the sword; and you will dash their children, and rip open their women with child."

So Hazael said, "But what is your servant-a dog, that he should do this gross thing?" And Elisha answered, "The LORD has shown me that you will become king over Syria.

King Benhadad got sick and sent Hazael his servant to Elisha to enquire if he would recover. It was an opportunity God allowed for His Word to Elijah to come to pass through Elisha. Let's see it again in 2 Kings 8:13, "Elisha said, "The Lord has shown me that you will become King over Syria."

As God's Prophet, he was to anoint Hazael King over Syria.

It was Prophet Samuel that anointed Saul King over Israel (1Samuel10:1) and anointed David (1 Samuel16:13).

Elijah did not anoint Hazael and Jehu as kings over Syria and Israel. Therefore, when Elisha took over from Elijah, it was his duty to do so. He did not. Even when he encountered Hazael and God reminded him, he still did not.

Elisha may have decided against it because he discerned his intentions. Those intentions could have been taken care of by the anointing. God had a plan for choosing Hazael (see 1 Kings 19:16-17).

When David was anointed by Samuel, the Spirit of the Lord came upon him from that day forward. The same would have happened to Hazael. God who created Hazael chose him and commanded his prophet to go anoint him. However, they did not. That is disobedience to divine instructions and is a very costly mistake to make. No matter what Elisha saw, obeying God and anointing Hazael would have placed God in responsibility over Hazael's life.

1 Kings 19:15-17
15 Then the LORD said to him: "Go, return on your way to the Wilderness of Damascus; and when you arrive, anoint Hazael as king over Syria.
16 "Also you shall anoint Jehu the son of Nimshi as king over Israel. And Elisha the son of Shaphat of Abel Meholah you shall anoint as prophet in your place.
17 It shall be that whoever escapes the sword of Hazael, Jehu will kill; and whoever escapes the sword of Jehu, Elisha will kill.

2 Kings 8:13

13 So Hazael said, "But what is your servant-a dog, that he should do this gross thing?" And Elisha answered, "The LORD has shown me that you will become king over Syria".

God gave Elijah the command. He also gave Elisha the confirmation. However, Elisha failed.

GOD HATES AND ABHORS DISOBEDIENCE

1 Samuel 15:17-23

So Samuel said, "When you were little in your own eyes, were you not head of the tribes of Israel? And did not the LORD anoint you king over Israel?
Now the LORD sent you on a mission, and said, 'Go, and utterly destroy the sinners, the Amalekites, and fight against them until they are consumed.'
"Why then did you not obey the voice of the LORD? Why did you swoop down on the spoil, and do evil in the sight of the LORD?"
And Saul said to Samuel, "But I have obeyed the voice of the LORD, and gone on the mission on which the LORD sent me, and brought back Agag king of Amalek; I have utterly destroyed the Amalekites.
But the people took of the plunder, sheep and oxen, the best of the things which should have been utterly destroyed, to sacrifice to the LORD your God in Gilgal."
Then Samuel said: "Has the LORD as great delight in burnt offerings and sacrifices, As in obeying the voice of the LORD? Behold, to obey is better than sacrifice, And to heed than the fat of rams.

For rebellion is as the sin of witchcraft, And stubbornness is as iniquity and idolatry. Because you have rejected the word of the LORD, He also has rejected you from being king."

Like Samuel, God sent Elisha on a mission but he disobeyed. Had Prophet Elisha anointed Hazael, God would have secured and redirected him to do well. Elisha did not believe God to change Hazael. Therefore, he refused to anoint him.

I believe the Lord permitted King Benhadad's sickness to occasion Elisha and Hazael's meeting for Elisha to anoint Hazael. Nevertheless, Elisha failed to obey God.

No matter how evil a man is, the anointing (Spirit of God) on the person will turn him into a different man.

God turned Saul the son of Kish into a different man after he was anointed
1 Samuel 10:1,6
Then Samuel took a flask of oil and poured it on his head, and kissed him and said: "Is it not because the LORD has anointed you commander over His inheritance?
Then the Spirit of the LORD will come upon you, and you will prophesy with them and be turned into another man.

Saul the murderer who later became Paul the Apostle was changed into another man after his encounter with the anointed.
Acts 9:10-18

Now there was a certain disciple at Damascus named Ananias; and to him the Lord said in a vision, "Ananias." And he said, "Here I am, Lord."

So the Lord said to him, "Arise and go to the street called Straight, and inquire at the house of Judas for one called Saul of Tarsus, for behold, he is praying.

And in a vision he has seen a man named Ananias coming in and putting his hand on him, so that he might receive his sight."

Then Ananias answered, "Lord, I have heard from many about this man, how much harm he has done to Your saints in Jerusalem.

And here he has authority from the chief priests to bind all who call on Your name."

But the Lord said to him, "Go, for he is a chosen vessel of Mine to bear My name before Gentiles, kings, and the children of Israel.

For I will show him how many things he must suffer for My name's sake."

And Ananias went his way and entered the house; and laying his hands on him he said, "Brother Saul, the Lord Jesus, who appeared to you on the road as you came, has sent me that you may receive your sight and be filled with the Holy Spirit."

Immediately there fell from his eyes something like scales, and he received his sight at once; and he arose and was baptized.

God can change anyone. I know Hazael will not have gone to murder King Benhadad if Elisha had anointed him King over Syria. However, Elisha refused anointing Hazael King. Therefore, God did not heal Elisha for his flagrant disobedience to heavenly commands and instructions.

Elisha anointed Jehu but did not anoint Hazael.

2 Kings 9 1-3, 4-6

And Elisha the prophet called one of the sons of the prophets, and said to him, "Get yourself ready, take this flask of oil in your hand, and go to Ramoth Gilead.

Now when you arrive at that place, look there for Jehu the son of Jehoshaphat, the son of Nimshi, and go in and make him rise up from among his associates, and take him to an inner room.

Then take the flask of oil, and pour it on his head, and say, 'Thus says the LORD: "I have anointed you king over Israel."' Then open the door and flee, and do not delay."

So the young man, the servant of the prophet, went to Ramoth Gilead.

And when he arrived, there were the captains of the army sitting; and he said, "I have a message for you, Commander." Jehu said, "For which one of us?" And he said, "For you, Commander."

Then he arose and went into the house. And he poured the oil on his head, and said to him, "Thus says the LORD God of Israel: 'I have anointed you king over the people of the LORD, over Israel.

Elisha enforced the anointing of Jehu King over Israel. He ought to have ensured Hazael was anointed King over Syria. You will not see where the Lord personally told Elisha to anoint Jehu in the Bible. Being God's Prophet in Elijah's place he was aware of the duty God gave Elijah and he did it. Had he believed God fully to handle Hazael, he would have anointed Haxael in obedience to God also, but he disobeyed.

So many Ministers' of God today have chosen to disobey the Lord's instructions and occasioned the death of the sick. And have reaped the fruit of their deeds through sickness and death. Hear what Elisha said:

"So Hazael went to meet him and took a present with him, of every good thing of Damascus, forty camel-loads; and he came and stood before him, and said, "Your son Ben-Hadad king of Syria has sent me to you, saying, 'Shall I recover from this disease?'"

And Elisha said to him, "Go, say to him, 'You shall certainly recover.' However the LORD has shown me that he will really die." 2 Kings 8:9-10

Had Elisha obeyed God's command, and anointed Hazael King over Syria, he would not have murdered King Benhadad and he would have recovered as God said. Elisha's willful act of disobedience caused the death of King Benhadad through Hazael even after God has said he will recover.

The Lord first's and last command to us is to preach the gospel of the Kingdom and to heal the sick.
Mathew 10:1
And when He had called His twelve disciples to Him, He gave them power over unclean spirits, to cast them out, and to heal all kinds of sickness and all kinds of disease.

Luke 9:1
Then He called His twelve disciples together and gave them power and authority over all demons, and to cure diseases.

Luke 10: 1, 8-9

1 After these things the Lord appointed seventy others also, and sent them two by two before His face into every city and place where He Himself was about to go.

8 "Whatever city you enter, and they receive you, eat such things as are set before you.

9 "And heal the sick there, and say to them, 'The kingdom of God has come near to you.'

Mark 16:15-18

15 And He said to them, "Go into all the world and preach the gospel to every creature.

16 "He who believes and is baptized will be saved; but he who does not believe will be condemned.

17 And these signs will follow those who believe: In My name they will cast out demons; they will speak with new tongues;

18 They will take up serpents; and if they drink anything deadly, it will by no means hurt them; they will lay hands on the sick, and they will recover."

Are you obedient to His commands? Are you involved in executing His mandate to His Church upon the earth?

Had Elisha anointed Hazael King over Syria, he could have averted the death of the King God said will recover. But Elisha's sentiments would not allow him. He disobeyed and his disobedient greatly contributed to his sickness and death.

CHAPTER FOUR

WHY ELISHA DIED SICK

It is never God's plan for any person to die sick. I want you to hear me and hear me clearly: God's plan is never for man to leave this earth because of sickness.

Death through sickness is a curse. It is not a blessing. Yet Elisha died sick.

2 Kings 13:14
Elisha had become sick with the illness of which he would die. Then Joash the king of Israel came down to him, and wept over his face, and said, "O my father, my father, the chariots of Israel and their horsemen!"

What made Elisha to die sick? Let us again
see why these two kings died!

1. The King of Israel died sick
2 Kings 1:1-4
1 Moab rebelled against Israel after the death of Ahab.

2 Now Ahaziah fell through the lattice of his upper room in Samaria, and was injured; so he sent messengers and said to them, "Go, inquire of Baal-Zebub, the god of Ekron, whether I shall recover from this injury."
3 But the angel of the LORD said to Elijah the Tishbite, "Arise, go up to meet the messengers of the king of Samaria, and say to them, 'Is it because there is no God in Israel that you are going to inquire of Baal-Zebub, the god of Ekron?'
4 "Now therefore, thus says the LORD: 'You shall not come down from the bed to which you have gone up, but you shall surely die.'" So Elijah departed.

2. The King of Judah died sick
2 Chronicles16:12-13
12 And in the thirty-ninth year of his reign, Asa became diseased in his feet, and his malady was severe; yet in his disease he did not seek the LORD, but the physicians.
13 So Asa rested with his fathers; he died in the forty-first year of his reign.

Jeremiah 17:5
5 Thus says the LORD: "Cursed is the man who trusts in man And makes flesh his strength, Whose heart departs from the LORD.

Both Israel's and Judah's Kings died because they sought not the Lord when they were sick.

Is it not clear from the above scriptures that anyone who does not seek the Lord while sick died? Who do you trust for your healing when sick? Do you seek the Lord. All who did were healed. Those who did not died. God respects no man's person.

1. Exodus 15:26
The Lord said, "If you diligently heed the voice of the LORD your God and do what is right in His sight, give ear to His commandments and keep all His statutes, I will put none of the diseases on you which I have brought on the Egyptians. For I am the LORD who heals you."

Give earnest heed to the voice of the LORD your God. To give ear to the voice of the Lord your God means to hear and obey or do what God's servants the Prophets tell you. I believe Elijah told Elisha why he was anointed as prophet in Elijah's office and about the anointing of Hazael and Jehu. He failed to anoint Hazael but anointed only Jehu. Half obedience is total disobedience. If you are guilty of one offence, you are guilty of all
James 2:10
For whoever shall keep the whole law, and yet stumble in one point, he is guilty of all.

Elisha did not obey the voice of the Lord God and had to pay for it.

Deuteronomy 28:1-3
1 Now it shall come to pass, if you diligently obey the voice of the LORD your God, to observe carefully all His commandments which I command you today, that the LORD your God will set you high above all nations of the earth.

2 And all these blessings shall come upon you and overtake you, because you obey the voice of the LORD your God:
3 Blessed shall you be in the city, and blessed shall you be in the country.

God says 'Blessed shall you be'. Sickness is not part of the "Blessed shall you be…."
The curses are listed in the second part of Deuteronomy chapter 28.
All the sickness and diseases people are suffering and many others not yet known are on 'the curse' part. Whether the blessing or the curse is dependent on what those who heard Moses (God's Voice) did. Therefore, Elisha died sick because he did not give earnest heed to the voice of the Lord God as stated clearly in the scriptures.

2 Kings 8:13
13 So Hazael said, "But what is your servant - a dog, that he should do this gross thing?" And Elisha answered, "The LORD has shown me that you will become king over Syria."

1 Kings 19:15-17
15 Then the LORD said to him: "Go, return on your way to the Wilderness of Damascus; and when you arrive, anoint Hazael as king over Syria.
16 "Also you shall anoint Jehu the son of Nimshi as king over Israel. And Elisha the son of Shaphat of Abel Meholah you shall anoint as prophet in your place.
17 "It shall be that whoever escapes the sword of Hazael, Jehu will kill; and whoever escapes the sword of Jehu, Elisha will kill.

God promised not to permit any of His obedient children suffer sickness. Why must his prophet be the one to suffer and die because of it? Elisha, and not God, was responsible for his sickness and death.

Exodus 15:26

"If you diligently heed the voice of the LORD your God and do what is right in His sight, give ear to His commandments and keep all His statutes, I will put none of the diseases on you which I have brought on the Egyptians. For I am the LORD who heals you."

1. Give earnest heed to the voice of the Lord
2. God says do what is right in His sight
3. Give ear to His Commandment
4. And keep all His statutes.
Then He becomes "The Lord Your Healer"

'The Lord our healer' cannot be Elisha's healer and sickness will take his life. God backed out of the deal because Elisha contravened the covenant or agreement.

2. Deuteronomy 7:11-15

11 Therefore you shall keep the commandment, the statutes, and the judgments, which I command you today, to observe them.
12 Then it shall come to pass, because you listen to these judgments, and keep and do them, that the LORD your God will keep with you the covenant and the mercy which He swore to your fathers.
13 And He will love you and bless you and multiply you; He will also bless the fruit of your womb and the fruit of your land, your grain and your new wine and your oil, the

increase of your cattle and the offspring of your flock, in the land of which He swore to your fathers to give you.

14 You shall be blessed above all peoples; there shall not be a male or female barren among you or among your livestock.

15 And the LORD will take away from you all sickness, and will afflict you with none of the terrible diseases of Egypt which you have known, but will lay them on all those who hate you.

1 – Keep the commandment

2 – Keep the statutes

3 – Keep the judgments

4 – And do them (the commandment, statutes and judgments).

If anyone does so, God who cannot lie shows what He will do. The last Word God says he will perform is clearly written in verse 15, "And the LORD will remove from you all sickness, and He will not put on you any of the harmful diseases of Egypt which you have known; but He will put them on all who hate you."

If God did not remove the sickness from Prophet Elisha's body till the sickness killed him, blame Elisha and not My Father. He (Elisha) missed it. He failed to keep and do the commandment of the LORD.

3. Exodus 23:25-26

25 So you shall serve the LORD your God, and He will bless your bread and your water. And I will take sickness away from the midst of you.

26 No one shall suffer miscarriage or be barren in your land; I will fulfill the number of your days.

1– Serve the Lord your God

2 – And He will remove sickness from your midst

3 – And He will fulfill the number of your days

Did Elisha serve God acceptably? You might be quick to say yes. But if he did, then God must have told a lie by saying "He will remove sickness from His servants and that He will fulfill the number of their days and then failed to do as He said." If God said He will do something if we do as He commands, He will unfailing do it. But if He fails to do it, then we actually forced Him not to keep His word by our disobedience or disloyalty.

If God did not remove sickness from Elisha's body nor fulfill the number of his days, then Elisha's service was not acceptable to God.

The question now is: *How do I serve God acceptably so that He will remove sickness from my body and fulfill the number of my days?*

1. Be willing and obedient to His commands, statutes and instructions.
Isaiah 1:18-19
18 Come now, and let us reason together," Says the LORD, "Though your sins are like scarlet, They shall be as white as snow; Though they are red like crimson, They shall be as wool.
19 If you are willing and obedient, You shall eat the good of the land;

2. Be completely obedient to All of His commands, statutes and instructions in your service if you want to enjoy all round prosperity.
Job 36:11

If they obey and serve Him, They shall spend their days in prosperity, And their years in pleasures.

<u>Psalms 35:27</u>
27 Let them shout for joy and be glad, Who favor my righteous cause; And let them say continually, "Let the LORD be magnified, Who has pleasure in the prosperity of His servant."

3. Serve God with joy and gladness of heart and do all He commands even when it makes no sense to you.
<u>Psalms 100:2-3</u>
2 Serve the LORD with gladness; Come before His presence with singing.
3 Know that the LORD, He is God; It is He who has made us, and not we ourselves; We are His people and the sheep of His pasture.

<u>Deuteronomy 28:47-48</u>
47 Because you did not serve the LORD your God with joy and gladness of heart, for the abundance of everything,
48 Therefore you shall serve your enemies, whom the LORD will send against you, in hunger, in thirst, in nakedness, and in need of everything; and He will put a yoke of iron on your neck until He has destroyed you.
No matter your service to God, if it is not offered with joy and gladness God does not accept it.

Elisha could still have anointed Hazael although what he saw was negative and contrary. The anointing would have changed Hazael as it did Saul and God's plan and purpose would have been accomplished as He had Hazael in His programme.

1 Kings 19:17

"It shall be that whoever escapes the sword of Hazael, Jehu will kill; and whoever escapes the sword of Jehu, Elisha will kill.

In *1 Samuel 10:1, 6Samuel anointed Saul and God took over Saul's life. "Then Samuel took a flask of oil and poured it on his head, and kissed him and said: "Is it not because the LORD has anointed you commander over His inheritance? Then the Spirit of the LORD will come upon you, and you will prophesy with them and be turned into another man."*

After Samuel anointed Saul, Scripture says, 'it was the Lord who anointed him.' And Saul was changed to a different man.

Many serve God but do so when what they see, hear, smell, taste or feel is in agreement with what they want God to do or what He says He will do.

Whether what our senses 'say' is in agreement with God's word or not, all God expects from us is to obey Him and walk by faith. I want to submit that Elisha, in the case of anointing Hazael, did not walk by faith and that was a costly mistake.

2 Corinthians 5:7

For we walk by faith, not by sight.

Habakkuk 2:4

Behold the proud, His soul is not upright in him; But the just shall live by his faith.

The just that fails to live by faith dies. Their death could be by sickness or disease, as in the case of Elisha or by any other means.

Please hear me: Believe God, walk, and live by faith. Whatever God commands, He wants us to obey. Whatever He instructs us to do through His servants (Human Agents), we must do.

If Elisha was anointed prophet in Elijah's room, office, place or position, he does not need to wait any moment after Elijah's departure to obey God and fulfill the unfulfilled job, task and responsibility God gave His master (Elijah) whom he served.

Elisha's failure to do this opened the door to the enemy who afflicted him with sickness that caused his eventual death prematurely.

We need to know what God wants us to do and do it as He has commanded if we want to avoid ending as Prophet Elisha did.

CHAPTER FIVE

LESSONS FROM ELISHA'S LIFE

Sickness is not God's will and can never be. It wastes. It destroys.

It is not God's will for any of His Children to die sick not to talk of His Prophets yet when His Prophets do wrong, they die as any other person.

If Elisha, whose dead, dry bones raised the dead, died sick, then anyone, just anyone can die sick.

God is no respecter of persons but respects His covenant and those who keep them.

God judges sin no matter how long it takes, particularly when one does not repent genuinely and return to God and His ways.

Disobedience no matter how trivial is costly, particularly to the ones God called to serve Him.

You are not too big as a minister for the enemy to waste your life as he can do to the ignorant.

You are not too big for God to secure you when you choose to go contrary to His statutes, commandment and instructions.

You must promptly obey God's instructions no matter how foolish they may appear.

1 Corinthians 1:25-29

25 The foolishness of God is wiser than men, and the weakness of God is stronger than men.

26 For you see your calling, brethren, that not many wise according to the flesh, not many mighty, not many noble, are called.

27 But God has chosen the foolish things of the world to put to shame the wise, and God has chosen the weak things of the world to put to shame the things which are mighty;

28 and the base things of the world and the things which are despised God has chosen, and the things which are not, to bring to nothing the things that are,

29 That no flesh should glory in His presence.

We have been given all we need to be free from sickness and live a fulfilled healthy sick free life by being obedient to God.

I have heard so many ministers in different ministries say when sick that God will heal them if He wants them healed. There's nothing farther away from the truth. If you are sick, you better go get your healing.

Listen if you don't do anything about your healing, God won't do anything either about it. It is unto you according to your faith.

Mathew 9:28-29

28 And when He had come into the house, the blind men came to Him. And Jesus said to them, "Do you believe that I am able to do this?" They said to Him, Yes, Lord."

29 Then He touched their eyes, saying, "According to your faith let it be to you.

Mark 5:34

And He said to her, "Daughter, your faith has made you well. Go in peace, and be healed of your affliction."

Mathew 15:28

Then Jesus answered and said to her, "O woman, great is your faith! Let it be to you as you desire." And her daughter was healed from that very hour.

God says "I am the Lord your healer" Again He says, "I will remove sickness from the midst of you and the number of your days I will fulfill. God cannot lie.

Number 23:19
God is not a man, that He should lie, Nor a son of man, that He should repent. Has He said, and will He not do? Or has He spoken, and will He not make it good?

Titus 1:2
in hope of eternal life which God, who cannot lie, promised before time began,

Hebrews 6:18
That by two immutable things, in which it is impossible for God to lie, we might have strong consolation, who have fled for refuge to lay hold of the hope set before us.

It is impossible for God to lie. Do not watch the enemy waste your life with sickness.
God has called us to glory and virtue. And your sickness cannot glorify God.
Even if nobody ever lived a sick free, healthy life, you can be the first. But thank God Moses and Elijah left this world without being sick. You will not die sick in Jesus Name.
You can learn from Elisha's case and take precautions. That is why this book. Learn, do and live!

CHAPTER SIX

HOW TO AVOID ELISHA'S MISTAKE

Elisha died sick and premature! But that is not God's plan for you. Elisha made a mistake and the devil took advantage of his mistake and struck him with sickness.

Job made a mistake and the devil struck him with sickness. Many people do not know that Job made a mistake but the Scripture shows his mistake in Job 3:25, *"For the thing I greatly feared has come upon me, And what I dreaded has happened to me."*

Why did Job live in constant fear until the enemy attacked. God shows us:
Job 1:5

So it was, when the days of feasting had run their course, that Job would send and sanctify them, and he would rise early in the morning and offer burnt offerings according to the number of them all. For Job said, "It may be that my sons have sinned and cursed God in their hearts." Thus Job did regularly.

Job 2:7

So Satan went out from the presence of the LORD, and struck Job with painful boils from the sole of his foot to the crown of his head.

Job confessed negatively, acted in fear regularly, and opened the door to the devil instead of opening the door for the Lord through faith.

Job realized his mistake, repented and got back into fellowship with God by faith. God instructed him to pray for his friends. Job obeyed and God healed and restored him

Job 42:10

10 And the LORD restored Job's losses when he prayed for his friends. Indeed the LORD gave Job twice as much as he had before.

Hezekiah did wrong and so was struck with sickness that almost cost him his life. What did he do wrong?

Hezekiah did not give to God what belongs to Him.

2 Chronicles 32:22, 25

22 Thus the LORD saved Hezekiah and the inhabitants of Jerusalem from the hand of Sennacherib the king of Assyria, and from the hand of all others, and guided them on every side.

25 But Hezekiah did not repay according to the favor shown him, for his heart was lifted up; therefore wrath was looming over him and over Judah and Jerusalem.

What did Hezekiah do when he was sick and was told he was to die?

Hezekiah repented and turned to God immediately and God healed him.

Isaiah 38:1-6

1 In those days Hezekiah was sick and near death. And Isaiah the prophet, the son of Amoz, went to him and said to him, "Thus says the LORD: 'Set your house in order, for you shall die and not live."

2 Then Hezekiah turned his face toward the wall, and prayed to the LORD,

3 and said, "Remember now, O LORD, I pray, how I have walked before You in truth and with a loyal heart, and have done what is good in Your sight." And Hezekiah wept bitterly.

4 And the word of the LORD came to Isaiah, saying,

5 Go and tell Hezekiah, 'Thus says the LORD, the God of David your father: "I have heard your prayer, I have seen your tears; surely I will add to your days fifteen years.

6 "I will deliver you and this city from the hand of the king of Assyria, and I will defend this city."'

Immediately Hezekiah turned back to God in repentance, he was gloriously healed. Isaiah was still within the courts of Hezekiah the King when He (God) sent him back to Hezekiah.

If Job and Hezekiah did not die sick, then there is no reason why God would not have healed Elisha if he did as he ought to have done.

Elisha caused whatever made God not to have healed him.

How can you avoid this mistake and live sickfree to accomplish your own purpose? How can you live and hand over successfully to another and not die through sickness or accidentally?

How can you finish your assignment and go back to heaven fulfilled and accomplished?

How can you ensure that not one of your days is lost to the devil and his cohorts?

I want to show you what the Lord taught me. Do them and you will live?

1. Never be bitter no matter what.
2. Always have a heart of forgiveness.

Mathew 6:14-15

14 For if you forgive men their trespasses, your heavenly Father will also forgive you.

15 But if you do not forgive men their trespasses, neither will your Father forgive your trespasses.

3. Control your anger when provoked and guard your tongue so that you won't say what is wrong and negative.

2 Kings 13:14-19

14 Elisha had become sick with the illness of which he would die. Then Joash the king of Israel came down to him, and wept over his face, and said, "O my father, my father, the chariots of Israel and their horsemen!"

15 And Elisha said to him, "Take a bow and some arrows." So he took himself a bow and some arrows.

16 Then he said to the king of Israel, "Put your hand on the bow." So he put his hand on it, and Elisha put his hands on the king's hands.

17 And he said, "Open the east window"; and he opened it. Then Elisha said, "Shoot"; and he shot. And he said, "The arrow of the LORD'S deliverance and the arrow of deliverance from Syria; for you must strike the Syrians at Aphek till you have destroyed them."

18 Then he said, "Take the arrows"; so he took them. And he said to the king of Israel, "Strike the ground"; so he struck three times, and stopped.

19 And the man of God was angry with him, and said, "You should have struck five or six times; then you would have struck Syria till you had destroyed it! But now you will strike Syria only three times."

Ecclesiastes 7:9, 17
9 Do not hasten in your spirit to be angry, For anger rests in the bosom of fools.

17 Do not be overly wicked, Nor be foolish: Why should you die before your time?

Outburst of Anger is a display of foolishness and leads to premature death.

4 Avoid overwork
Philippians 2:25-27
25 Yet I considered it necessary to send to you Epaphroditus, my brother, fellow worker, and fellow soldier, but your messenger and the one who ministered to my need;

26 since he was longing for you all, and was distressed because you had heard that he was sick.
27 For indeed he was sick almost unto death; but God had mercy on him, and not only on him but on me also, lest I should have sorrow upon sorrow.

5. Have helpers you can delegate work to; train and empower them to help you.

6. Don't operate alone.

7. If sick, seek God for healing and ensure you forgive all who offended you.

8. Never relax and wait for God to heal you if He wants. Seek Him for your healing now.

9. Be very prompt in your obedience the moment you are certain of what God wants you to do.

10. Do what God commands always and never entertain any kind of fear no matter the threats against your life.

2 Kings 8: 1, 7

1 Then Elisha spoke to the woman whose son he had restored to life, saying, "Arise and go, you and your household, and stay wherever you can; for the LORD has called for a famine, and furthermore, it will come upon the land for seven years."
7 Then Elisha went to Damascus, and Ben-Hadad king of Syria was sick; and it was told him, saying, "The man of God has come here."

Afterwards, Elisha left for Damascus and hid himself. Fear was the major reason for his move.

Jehu was to be anointed King and Elisha ought to anoint Jehu by himself. But for fear, he couldn't. Even when he sent a servant to go do his job for him, he took 'fearful precautions'.

2 Kings 9 1-3, 4-6
1 And Elisha the prophet called one of the sons of the prophets, and said to him, "Get yourself ready, take this flask of oil in your hand, and go to Ramoth Gilead.
2 Now when you arrive at that place, look there for Jehu the son of Jehoshaphat, the son of Nimshi, and go in and make him rise up from among his associates, and take him to an inner room.
3 Then take the flask of oil, and pour it on his head, and say, 'Thus says the LORD: "I have anointed you king over Israel."' Then open the door and flee, and do not delay."

Elisha was indeed afraid. Job feared and he was struck with sickness.
Elisha feared also and became vulnerable to satanic attack with sickness. He opened the door and Satan visited.

The Lord commands us not to fear.

Mathew 10:28
"And do not fear those who kill the body but cannot kill the soul. But rather fear Him who is able to destroy both soul and body in hell.

Jesus said we must not fear him who can kill the body and cannot touch the soul. Only God who has power to kill both the body and destroy the soul in fire is to be feared.
Elisha ought to have anointed both Hazael and Jehu personally as God's Prophet in Elijah's office. But he didn't. For Hazael, we saw the reason in 2Kings 8:11-13,

80

"Then he set his countenance in a stare until he was ashamed; and the man of God wept.

And Hazael said, "Why is my lord weeping?" He answered, "Because I know the evil that you will do to the children of Israel: Their strongholds you will set on fire, and their young men you will kill with the sword; and you will dash their children, and rip open their women with child."

So Hazael said, "But what is your servant-a dog, that he should do this gross thing?" And Elisha answered, "The LORD has shown me that you will become king over Syria."

But why didn't Elisha God's prophet anoint Jehu as King over Israel? Why did he send someone to go and do it when he was still healthy, sound and vibrant?

The simple reason was fear. Elisha was afraid of being killed. The king of Israel vowed to kill him

2 Kings 6:30-32

30 Now it happened, when the king heard the words of the woman, that he tore his clothes; and as he passed by on the wall, the people looked, and there underneath he had sackcloth on his body.

31 Then he said, "God do so to me and more also, if the head of Elisha the son of Shaphat remains on him today."

32 But Elisha was sitting in his house, and the elders were sitting with him. And the king sent a man ahead of him, but before the messenger came to him, he said to the elders, "Do you see how this son of a murderer has sent someone to take away my head? Look, when the messenger comes, shut the door, and hold him fast at the door. Is not the sound of his master's feet behind him?"

Why did the king of Israel vow to kill Elisha? Because he believed Elisha was responsible for the famine as God's prophet.

2 Kings 6:33

While Elisha was still saying this, the messenger arrived. And the king said, All this calamity is from the LORD; why should I wait for the LORD any longer?"

God has promised to preserve us.

Psalms 121:7-8

7 The LORD shall preserve you from all evil; He shall preserve your soul.

8 The LORD shall preserve your going out and your coming in From this time forth, and even forevermore.

1 Thessalonians 5:23

Now may the God of peace Himself sanctify you completely; and may your whole spirit, soul, and body be preserved blameless at the coming of our Lord Jesus Christ.

God preserved Jesus the prophet as he did Moses and Elijah, when threatened.

Luke 13:31-33

31 On that very day some Pharisees came, saying to Him, "Get out and depart from here, for Herod wants to kill You."

32 And He said to them, "Go, tell that fox, 'Behold, I cast out demons and perform cures today and tomorrow, and the third day I shall be perfected.'

33 Nevertheless I must journey today, tomorrow, and the day following; for it cannot be that a prophet should perish outside of Jerusalem.

This is the word of the LORD to His servants:
Luke 12:4-5
4 And I say to you, My friends, do not be afraid of those who kill the body, and after that have no more that they can do.
5 But I will show you whom you should fear: Fear Him who, after He has killed, has power to cast into hell; yes, I say to you, fear Him!

You must not be afraid of death for God can preserve you from death at any time, anywhere, under any circumstance. Elisha feared death by a man and death came by sickness. He feared death and death came. It was fear that opened the door to the enemy who comes to steal, and to kill and to destroy.

To avoid Elisha mistake, fear not. Do not take step's based on fear. We walk by faith.
2 Corinthians 5:7
For we walk by faith, not by sight.

Faith is the key to our victory against all odds.
1 John 5:4
4 For whatever is born of God overcomes the world. And this is the victory that has overcome the world--our faith.

Take faith steps. Do not fear man who can kill the body and cannot touch your soul. Fear God and evil will fear you and bow to you.
To conquer fear, follow God by being obedient to His instructions.
 I Peter 3:13

And who is he who will harm you if you become followers of what is good?
Seek and do good and none can harm you.

Be willing to sacrifice your life for God and He will preserve you by all means.
Revelation 12:11
And they overcame him by the blood of the Lamb and by the word of their testimony, and they did not love their lives to the death.
Luke 9:24
"For whoever desires to save his life will lose it, but whoever loses his life for My sake will save it.
Luke 17:33
"Whoever seeks to save his life will lose it, and whoever loses his life will preserve it.

Elisha became sick and died because he was afraid of death. He chose to keep himself by going into hiding when He had not done what he was commanded to do as God's prophet.
Many chosen ministers of God have gone to hide in jobs to make more money for fear of lack. Watch them and see how they end!
Some have not believed nor received the Lord as their Healer but have doctors they consult when sick. God's chosen ones are afraid that God cannot keep them after all. Therefore, they have taken steps to keep themselves. And the result is sudden death, whether through sickness, disease, murder or oppression. They have ended dead!

JESUS IS YOUR HEALER

I remember reading the testimony of Dr. A.B. Simpson, founder of the Christian Missionary Alliance. He was a Presbyterian minister and pastor, and in his mid-forties, he developed a serious heart condition. The best specialist of that day said nothing could be done for Him.

Dr. Simpson knew nothing at all about the subject of healing. He had never examined the Bible on that subject, even though he was a minister of the Gospel and a graduate of a seminary. Now many in his own Presbyterian church congregation had testified of being healed. And he knew they were healed, because he knew something about their conditions.

So he decided to take a leave of absence from his church and go back to his farm, where every single day, he spent ten to twelve hours examining the Scripture on the subject of healing. He would take his Bible and a notebook and get away from the house. He would sit in the sunshine under a tree, out in the fresh air. He would lean back against the tree with his Bible and notebook and make notes.

After two weeks of doing that, he became convinced that divine healing belonged to him. So without being any better, with all his heart symptoms, he wrote down the following: Having studied the word of God and having come to see that healing for the physical body is ours today just as much as the remission and forgiveness of sins, I now accept Jesus as my Healer.

BELIEVE THE TRUTH
Some time later, Dr. A. B. Simpson was invited to speak at a luncheon. He preached from Matthew 8:17: "Himself (Jesus) took our infirmities and bare our sicknesses." He

told the people at the luncheon that he had heard it preached all his life that "Himself took our sins," but during his intensive two-weeks study of the Bible, he had come to see that "Himself also took our infirmities and bare our sicknesses."

Then he said, "I'm in my mid-forties, but I want you to know that Himself took my disease and my heart condition. Therefore, I don't have them anymore." When he said that, he still felt weak. He knew his heart was still not beating right.

His head said, "You've played the fool. You got up and told these folks that you're healed and that Jesus took your infirmities. But you're still got them."

But on the inside of him(that's where you have to believe God-on the inside of you), he said, "Devil, according to Matthew 8:17, I'm healed, because Himself took infirmities and bore my sicknesses." Then his strength came to him and his heart rhythm straightened out. He started to feel good.

Believing the truth found in the word of God, Dr. A. B. Simpson was completely healed!

The decision and action brought him into a covenant with the Lord not just for his personal healing and preservation but for that of his entire family.
Beloved, it works.

Fear not! He that keeps you does not sleep nor slumber. He is able to keep to the uttermost those who come to Him and depend on Him for their safety. You will not die. Only Believe and live! Again, I say to you, fear not, no matter the threat on your life from the enemy. You are so precious to God that He will not watch the enemy use sickness to destroy your life.

A.B. Simpson's Testimony is taken from
Health Food By Kenneth E Hagin.

CHAPTER SEVEN

WHAT IT TAKES TO BE SICKFREE

God does not want you sick. Hear what He says, *"For I will restore health to you And heal you of your wounds,' says the LORD,* 'Because they called you an outcast saying: "This is Zion; No one seeks her." Jeremiah 30:17 "If you diligently heed the voice of the LORD your God and do what is right in His sight, give ear to His commandments and keep all His statutes, I will put none of

87

the diseases on you which I have brought on the Egyptians. *For I am the LORD who heals you."* Exodus 15:26

"I will restore health to you and heal you...for I am the LORD that heals you."
The Lord has been in this business of healing and is still on it.
Acts 10:38
"how God anointed Jesus of Nazareth with the Holy Spirit and with power, who went about doing good and healing all who were oppressed by the devil, for God was with Him.

Jesus died to free you from sickness forever.

1 Peter 2:24
Who Himself bore our sins in His own body on the tree, that we, having died to sins, might live for righteousness-- by whose stripes you were healed.

Jesus took our disease and bore our sickness and we cannot have or bear them again.
Mathew 8:17
That it might be fulfilled which was spoken by Isaiah the prophet, saying: "He Himself took our infirmities And bore our sicknesses."

God has done what He must do to keep us healthy.
Psalms 107:20
He sent His word and healed them, And delivered them from their destructions.

God has given to us His Eternal medicine to take always.

Proverbs 4:20-22

20 My son, give attention to my words; Incline your ear to my sayings.

21 Do not let them depart from your eyes; Keep them in the midst of your heart;

22 For they are life to those who find them, And health (Medicine) to all their flesh.

God wants you sickfree. It is not God's will for you to be sick no matter who you are, or what you have done.

God did not permit wicked enemies of His people to die sick.

Benhadad, king of Syria who made wars against Israel, God's chosen people got sick and when he enquired of God, God said he will recover.

2 Kings 6:8

Now the king of Syria was making war against Israel; and he consulted with his servants, saying, "My camp will be in such and such a place."

Not only did Benhadad war against Israel, he sent his men to kidnap Elisha, God's Prophet.

2 Kings 6:12-13

12 And one of his servants said, "None, my lord, O king; but Elisha, the prophet who is in Israel, tells the king of Israel the words that you speak in your bedroom."

13 So he said, "Go and see where he is, that I may send and get him." And it was told him, saying, "Surely he is in Dothan."

Benhadad, yet again besieged Samaria and caused a famine and hardship till two women killed and ate up a child of God.

2 Kings 6:24-29

24 And it happened after this that Ben-Hadad king of Syria gathered all his army, and went up and besieged Samaria.

25 And there was a great famine in Samaria; and indeed they besieged it until a donkey's head was sold for eighty shekels of silver, and one-fourth of a kab of dove droppings for five shekels of silver.

26 Then, as the king of Israel was passing by on the wall, a woman cried out to him, saying, "Help, my lord, O king!"

27 And he said, "If the LORD does not help you, where can I find help for you? From the threshing floor or from the winepress?"

28 Then the king said to her, "What is troubling you?" And she answered, "This woman said to me, 'Give your son, that we may eat him today, and we will eat my son tomorrow.'

29 "So we boiled my son, and ate him. And I said to her on the next day, 'Give your son, that we may eat him'; but she has hidden her son."

This Benhadad got sick and sent to enquire of God through Elisha the Prophet of God whether he will recover. And God says, "You will recover"

2 Kings 8:7-10, 14

7 Then Elisha went to Damascus and Ben-Hadad king of Syria was sick; and it was told him, saying, "The man of God has come here."

8 And the king said to Hazael, "Take a present in your hand, and go to meet the man of God, and inquire of the LORD by him, saying, 'Shall I recover from this disease?'"

9 So Hazael went to meet him and took a present with him, of every good thing of Damascus, forty camel-loads; and he came and stood before him, and said, "Your son Ben-

Hadad king of Syria has sent me to you, saying, 'Shall I recover from this disease?'"
10 And Elisha said to him, "Go, say to him, 'You shall certainly recover.' However the LORD has shown me that he will really die."
14 Then he departed from Elisha, and came to his master, who said to him, "What did Elisha say to you?" And he answered, "He told me you would surely recover."

If God through Elisha said that king Benhadad would recover, why should anyone die sick? Why must God's children or anyone else not be healed and preserved sickfree?

Hear me please: It is God's will for you to be sickfree. And you will be healed today if you are sick in Jesus Name.

WHAT MUST YOU DO TO BE FREE FROM SICKNESS?

1. Know and believe sickness is not God's will for you or for anyone.
3 John 2
Beloved, I pray that you may prosper in all things and be in health, just as your soul prospers.

2. Search your heart and see if you transgressed in any way and get back into fellowship with God immediately if sick.
Psalms 119:67
67 Before I was afflicted I went astray, But now I keep Your word.
Psalms 107:17-20

17 Fools, because of their transgression, And because of their iniquities, were afflicted.

18 Their soul abhorred all manner of food, And they drew near to the gates of death.

19 Then they cried out to the LORD in their trouble, And He saved them out of their distresses.

20 He sent His word and healed them, And delivered them from their destructions.

3. If sick, believe Healing is God's will now.
Jeremiah 30:17
17 For I will restore health to you And heal you of your wounds,' says the LORD, 'Because they called you an outcast saying: "This is Zion; No one seeks her."'
John 6:38
"For I have come down from heaven, not to do My own will, but the will of Him who sent Me.
Acts 10:38
"how God anointed Jesus of Nazareth with the Holy Spirit and with power, who went about doing good and healing all who were oppressed by the devil, for God was with Him.

4. Seek the word of God for your healing today by locating God's Messengers sent to bring healing and listen to their words and teachings. Always remember that God heals by sending His word to you first. Until you get His word and teachings, you are not ready for His healing.
Isaiah 30:20-21
20 And though the Lord gives you the
Bread of adversity and the water of affliction, Yet your teachers will not be moved into a corner anymore, But your eyes shall see your teachers.

21 Your ears shall hear a word behind you, saying, "This is the way, walk in it," Whenever you turn to the right hand Or whenever you turn to the left.

Psalms 107:20

He sent His word and healed them, And delivered them from their destructions.

5. Obey every healing Scripture and instructions they give you.

Proverb 4:20-22

20 My son, give attention to my words; Incline your ear to my sayings.

21 Do not let them depart from your eyes; Keep them in the midst of your heart;

22 For they are life to those who find them, And health (Medicine) to all their flesh.

6. Fill your heart with healing Scripture and speak it always over yourself always.

Proverbs 4:20-23

20 My son, give attention to my words;
Incline your ear to my sayings.

21 Do not let them depart from your eyes; Keep them in the midst of your heart;

22 For they are life to those who find them, And health (Medicine) to all their flesh.

23 Keep your heart with all diligence, For out of it spring the issues of life.

Romans 1:16

For I am not ashamed of the gospel of Christ, for it is the power of God to salvation for everyone who believes, for the Jew first and also for the Greek.

Romans 10:8-10

8 "The word is near you, in your mouth and in your heart" (that is, the word of faith which we preach):

9 that if you confess with your mouth the Lord Jesus and believe in your heart that God has raised Him from the dead, you will be saved.

10 For with the heart one believes unto righteousness and with the mouth confession is made unto salvation.

7. Accept The Lord as your Healer, ask Him for your Healing now.

Exodus 15:26

26 And He said, "If you diligently heed the voice of the LORD your God and do what is right in His sight, give ear to His commandments and keep all His statutes, I will put none of the diseases on you which I have brought on the Egyptians. For I am the LORD who heals you."

Malachi 3:6

6 For I am the LORD, I do not change; Therefore you are not consumed, O sons of Jacob.

8. Believe That God heard and has healed you and Receive your healing by faith and thank Him for it.

Mark 11:22-24

22 So Jesus answered and said to them, "Have faith in God.

23 "For assuredly, I say to you, whoever says to this mountain, 'Be removed and be cast into the sea,' and does not doubt in his heart, but believes that those things he says will be done, he will have whatever he says.

24 "Therefore I say to you, whatever things you ask when you pray, believe that you receive them, and you will have them.

HAVING RECEIVED YOUR HEALING, HOW DO YOU RETAIN IT AND BE HEALTHY?

i. Seek and maintain fellowship with God and the brethren. Never isolate yourself from others if you want to enjoy His Life.

Hebrews 10:25

25 Not forsaking the assembling of ourselves together, as is the manner of some, but exhorting one another, and so much the more as you see the Day approaching.

Psalms 133: 1-3

1 Behold, how good and how pleasant it is For brethren to dwell together in unity!

2 It is like the precious oil upon the head, Running down on the beard, The beard of Aaron, Running down on the edge of his garments.

3 It is like the dew of Hermon, Descending upon the mountains of Zion; For there the LORD commanded the blessing even Life forevermore.

ii. Live and walk by faith and never allow your senses to cause you to err.

Romans 1:16-17

16 For I am not ashamed of the gospel of Christ, for it is the power of God to salvation for everyone who believes, for the Jew first and also for the Greek.

17 For in it the righteousness of God is revealed from faith to faith; as it is written, "The just shall live by faith."

2 Corinthians 5:7

For we walk by faith, not by sight.

iii. Always speak healing and healthy Scriptures. Confess the following always.

"He Himself took our infirmities and bore our sicknesses." "And by His stripes you were healed." Mathew 8:17; 1Peter 2:24.

Hebrews 10:23

Let us hold fast the confession of our hope without wavering, for He who promised is faithful.

Revelation 12:11

They overcame him by the blood of the Lamb and by the word of their testimony, and they did not love their lives to the death.

iv. Hear and Hearken unto the voice of the Lord God by listening to teachings from healing messengers sent by Him.

Deuteronomy 11:26

Behold, I set before you today a blessing and a curse:

Deuteronomy 28:1-2

1 Now it shall come to pass, if you diligently obey the voice of the LORD your God, to observe carefully all His commandments which I command you today, that the LORD your God will set you high above all nations of the earth.

2 And all these blessings shall come upon you and overtake you, because you obey the voice of the LORD your God:

Exodus 15:26

26 and said, "If you diligently heed the voice of the LORD your God and do what is right in His sight, give ear to His commandments and keep all His statutes, I will put none of the diseases on you which I have brought on the Egyptians. For I am the LORD who heals you."

Like Moses, the Lord sent me as His mouthpiece to bring His Word to all. To receive my word is to receive His word and to reject my word is to reject His word.

v. Willingly obey and do the commandment, statutes and instructions that I bring to you.
Deuteronomy 7:11,15
11 Therefore you shall keep the commandment, the statutes, and the judgments which I command you today, to observe them.
15 And the LORD will take away from you all sickness, and will afflict you with none of the terrible diseases of Egypt which you have known, but will lay them on all those who hate you.

Job 36:11
11 If they obey and serve Him, They shall spend their days in prosperity, And their years in pleasures.

vi. Joyfully and gladly serve the Lord thy God all the days of your life no matter what others think, say or do.
Deuteronomy 28: 47-48
47 Because you did not serve the LORD your God with joy and gladness of heart, for the abundance of everything,
48 Therefore you shall serve your enemies, whom the LORD will send against you, in hunger, in thirst, in nakedness, and in need of everything; and He will put a yoke of iron on your neck until He has destroyed you.
Psalms 100:2-3
2 Serve the LORD with gladness; Come before His presence with singing.

3 Know that the LORD, He is God; It is He who has made us, and not we ourselves; We are His people and the sheep of His pasture.

Exodus 23:25-26

25 So you shall serve the LORD your God, and He will bless your bread and your water. And I will take sickness away from the midst of you.

26 No one shall suffer miscarriage or be barren in your land; I will fulfill the number of your days.

Psalms 91:16

16 With long life I will satisfy him, And show him My salvation."

vii. Stand your ground always

Ephesians 6:10, 13, 16

10 Finally, my brethren, be strong in the Lord and in the power of His might.

13 Therefore take up the whole armor of God, that you may be able to withstand in the evil day, and having done all, to stand.

16 above all, taking the shield of faith with which you will be able to quench all the fiery darts of the wicked one.

Remember that:

Jesus paid fully for your sickness.

1 Peter 4:1

Therefore, since Christ suffered for us in the flesh, arm yourselves also with the same mind, for he who has suffered in the flesh has ceased from sin,

1 Peter 2:24

Who Himself bore our sins in His own body on the tree, that we, having died to sins, might live for righteousness-- by whose stripes you were healed.

Jesus bore All your sicknesses and diseases
Isaiah 53:4-5
4 Surely He has borne our griefs And carried our sorrows; Yet we esteemed Him stricken, Smitten by God, and afflicted.
5 But He was wounded for our transgressions, He was bruised for our iniquities; The chastisement for our peace was upon Him, And by His stripes we are healed.
Mathew 8:17
That it might be fulfilled which was spoken by Isaiah the prophet, saying: "He Himself took our infirmities And bore our sicknesses."

Jesus has redeemed you from sickness and disease.
Deuteronomy 28:15, 61
15 But it shall come to pass, if you do not obey the voice of the LORD your God, to observe carefully all His commandments and His statutes which I command you today, that all these curses will come upon you and overtake you:
61 Also every sickness and every plague, which is not written in this Book of the Law, will the LORD bring upon you until you are destroyed.

Galatians 3:13-14
13 Christ has redeemed us from the curse of the law, having become a curse for us (for it is written, "Cursed is everyone who hangs on a tree"),

14 that the blessing of Abraham might come upon the Gentiles in Christ Jesus, that we might receive the promise of the Spirit through faith.

You now live in the Kingdom of Jesus Christ where no sickness is. So, Give thanks for your Health care package or inheritance

Colossians 1:12-14

12 giving thanks to the Father who has qualified us to be partakers of the inheritance of the saints in the light.

13 He has delivered us from the power of darkness and conveyed us into the kingdom of the Son of His love,

14 in whom we have redemption through His blood, the forgiveness of sins.

Revelation 5:9-10

9 And they sang a new song, saying: "You are worthy to take the scroll, And to open its seals; For You were slain, And have redeemed us to God by Your blood Out of every tribe and tongue and people and nation,

10 And have made us kings and priests to our God; And we shall reign on the earth."

You cannot reign with sickness in your body. Therefore, you cannot keep any sickness in you henceforth. I forbid it and declare you free now in Jesus Name.

CONCLUSION

Elisha died sick in spite of the anointing he had. To his bones, Elisha was anointed, yet he died sick.

This Publication is ordained of God to help you live and fulfill your destiny.

Please get the other titles in this family – "Why Christians Die sick" in spite of God's love and "Why Rich Christians Die Sick" in spite of their wealth, riches and prosperity, which is from the Lord.

Elisha died sick in spite of The Anointing he carried.

Christian Believers, God's Children, die sick in spite of God's love for them.

Rich Christians Die sick, in spite of their wealth which most of them got genuinely without enjoying it.

God does not want you to end in shame.

"A man who is in honour and does not know it is like a beast of the field that perishes" says God (Psalms 49:20)

You will not die premature.

You will not die sick.

You will not end in shame.

Your death will not bring reproach to God.

You will live and fulfill your life's purpose and destiny.

You will not die sick like Prophet Elisha in Jesus Name.

He gave me a commandment to bless you.

I decree you blessed.

I stop the curse of sickness on you now.

I unstop the blessing flow of healing and health. It is a new day for you now and evermore in Jesus Name.

Live and reign over sickness, disease and all evils.

God's Peace be yours and all that is yours in Jesus mighty Name.

I am expecting your testimonies.

Please write and share your testimonies with us.

If You are not certain that You are Born Again as you are certain about your name, or You were once saved but went astray again, living and doing as you pleased, Then say aloud this Prayer:

PRAYER FOR SALVATION AND RESTORATION!

Dear Heavenly Father, I return to you by Faith. I am sorry for my sins. I believe in my heart Jesus is The Christ and that He died for my sins and rose from the dead on the third day, according to Scripture, for my justification. I confess that Jesus Christ is LORD and I accept Him now as my Saviour. I believe my sins are wiped away.
I call upon The Name of The LORD for my total Healing, Liberty and Restoration.
I ask for the Gift of Your Holy Spirit, Power and Grace to follow and serve You from this day forward. And I Thank You Abba Father for doing far beyond all I have asked and can ever imagine in Jesus Name. Amen!
I NOW DECLARE THAT I AM A CHILD OF GOD FOREVER!

You can also Enlist now and become a Partner and or Member of our Totally Empowered Ambassadors on Mission (TEAM) and see what Our Risen Lord and King Jesus Christ will transform your life into and do in, for and through you from this day as believe and obey His Word!

ABOUT THE AUTHOR

Amb Promise Ogbonna

The Risen Lord Jesus Christ appointed and commissioned Amb Promise Ogbonna as His Official Ambassador and Living Witness and sent him with His Staff of Office to Prove to all worldwide that He is ALIVE TODAY! He is sent to Proclaim and Publish The Everlasting Gospel to every creature everywhere; To Stop anything after man's destruction; To Bring Healing, Liberty and Restoration to all; To Raise, Build and Plant all as Christ's Ambassadors on His Mission everywhere and Restore all things at all cost and by all means!

He is the President of Christ's Ambassadors Living Mission International Inc., an all-encompassing network of ministries and Lead Pastor of CHRIST'S AMBASSADORS - JESUS MISSION HEADQUARTERS, a non-denominational Assembly and Fellowship of Ambassadors and Citizens of Heaven on Christ's Mission worldwide.

As an Ambassador, He does not share his personal idea or opinion but Only speaks and Publishes The Everlasting Gospel and God's Wisdom that brings God's Solutions to every problem and challenges confronting mankind today! The Words he speaks or writes are not his words but The Words of His King and Lord Jesus Christ who is The Wisdom and Power of God. Therefore, His Books are not just to show people what belongs to them now but to restore whatever belongs to the people to them. To read his books is to receive God's answers to all of your questions and God's solutions to all of your problems!

He is married to Favour Promise, a trained Lawyer and they are blessed with four wonderful children.

Amb Promise Ogbonna

Christ's Ambassadors Living Mission Int'l - *Jesus Mission Headquarters*
WhatsApp or Text: **+2348060635805, +2348053995257, +2348027829586**
E-mail: ambpromiseo@gmail.com
Website: www.calm.org.ng.
Connect with Amb Promise on Facebook, Twitter, Instagram and on You Tube.
.

CHRIST'S AMBASSADORS LIVING MISSION INT'L - *JESUS MISSION HEADQUARTERS*
WELCOMES YOU TO THESE SPECIALIZED SERVICES

__Weekdays__: 12:00-1:00pm. Hour of EmPowerment for All
__Saturdays__: 8:00-9:00am. Hour of Healing & Freedom for All
__Sundays__: 8:00-9:00am. Hour of Liberty & Restoration for All
__Sundays__: 9:00-10:00am. Hour of Kingdom Wealth Transfer to All
__Last Friday Night Monthly:__ 10:00pm. Night of Restorations for All
__Ambassadors Bible Institute:__ Trains and Releases Christ's Ambassadors on His Mission everywhere! Enroll today!

Venue: 24 Independence Street, Behind O'MARK Schools by O'MARK Bus Stop, LASU Road, Igando Lagos.

OUR HEALING PRODUCTS AND SERVICES

1. All-Purpose Divine Healing Medicine
2. Healing Messages - CD, MP3 & DVD
3. Healing Books
4. Healing Leaves Magazine
5. Healing Anointing Oil
6. Healing Mantles & Clothes
7. Healing Materials
8. Healing Elixir for incurable diseases
9. Healing Songs
10. Healing Homes
11. Healing Seminars
12. Healing School
13. Healing Teams
14. Healing Outreaches & Explosions
15. World Healing Conferences
16. Health Centre
17. Healing Balm

We are on a Mission to free the World from all sicknesses and diseases and Restore ALL to God's Original Condition, Plan, Place and Purpose!

Call us now for our Healing Products and Services! We can't wait to SERVE YOU!

OTHER BOOKS BY AMB PROMISE OGBONNA
1. The Nothingness of Satan
2. You Can Make a Fresh Start
3. Restoring The Forgotten Dignity of Woman
4. Christ's Ambassadors: Raising Rulers in God's Own Very Class

5. Christ's Ambassadors: Building Rulers in God's Own Very Class

6. Christ's Ambassadors: Re-Emergence of Rulers in God's Own Very Class
**Christ's Ambassadors: Re-Emergence of Rulers in God's Own Very Class Handbook
7. Manifesting As Signs and Wonders.

8. 40 Pitfalls to Avoid.
9. Wisdom Seeds to Greatness In Life

Printed in Great Britain
by Amazon